"What a beautiful book, full of hope, pra[...] help navigate spiritual parenthood. I'm s[...] parents on how to approach spiritual pare[...], and invitations to freedom. It's not anxiety, fear, or shame that motivates, but the real hope of Jesus being present to our children, no matter their age, and in all the ways they are uniquely made. May we all be better equipped to love our children so that they may know the God who loves them, their friends, and their communities."

Sarah Shin, author of *Beyond Colorblind*

"We would have loved to have *Teach Your Children Well* when we were rearing our own children. This is a practical book, a boots-on-the-ground book, from a mother who has practiced what she is writing about. Sarah is funny, wise, thoughtful, and great with diagrams that provide a path forward in parenting the child you have. This is not about making the 'ideal Christian child.' It is about how you receive the child you were given so you can partner with God in growing, training, and celebrating this child. If you are looking for a theologically sound and developmentally savvy resource in your parenting, *Teach Your Children Well* is for you."

Doug and Adele Calhoun, coauthors of *Spiritual Rhythms for the Enneagram*

"*Teach Your Children Well* is written for anyone who knows a child. While aimed at parents, any adult who shares a passion for leading children into an adult relationship with Jesus can benefit from this content. Sarah understands the influence parents have on the direction of their children at every age and stage of their development. The reflection questions at the end of each chapter for parents, pastors, and church leaders provide a process moment for immediate practical application. My prayer along with Sarah's is that we indeed teach our children well."

Virginia Ward, dean of the Boston campus, Gordon-Conwell Theological Seminary

"This book is so chock-full of good ideas that they started falling out of the pages. A grace-filled reminder that when it comes to discipling children, there is no substitute for a parent. Amen to that."

Justin Whitmel Earley, business lawyer and author of *The Common Rule*

"If you are looking for a book that equips and empowers parents to train children for a life with God, this is it. Sarah Cowan Johnson brings together head and heart in this insightfully instructive manual for the discipleship of children and families. *Teach Your Children Well* is filled with creative ideas and authentic stories for every developmental stage."

Lacy Finn Borgo, author of *Spiritual Conversations with Children* and *All Will Be Well*

"Sarah Cowan Johnson's instincts are absolutely right: parents can be the most important pastoral presence in their child's life. Our children need something real to grab on to—from our own life with God, from their own encounters with God, and from the everyday moments when God is close. God is always very close to us. This book is a very practical guide helping parents facilitate the practice of encountering God in the tiny moments of everyday life. This book will absolutely help parents in the work of the spiritual accompaniment of their children."

Jared Patrick Boyd, author of *Imaginative Prayer: A Yearlong Guide to Your Child's Spiritual Formation*

"If we're honest, we've long outsourced much of what it means to raise our children to familiar institutions: schools, media, and churches. We don't mean to do this; it's simply the norm we've come to accept. As a result, even well-intentioned parents miss opportunities daily to form the hearts, minds, and faith of our children. In *Teach Your Children Well*, my friend Sarah Cowan Johnson offers a better path. Drawing on experiences from Johnson's pastoral and parenting life, this book provides strategies that are theologically robust and incredibly practical. This is a timely resource that will give parents the clarity and confidence to be the primary disciple makers of their children."

Shaun Marshall, pastor and author of *Transition Decisions: How to Get Unstuck, Embrace Change, and Make Your Next Move Now*

"For such a time as this, for such a world as this: *Teach Your Children Well* by Sarah Cowan Johnson is a timely book that will revolutionize how you parent your children and think about discipleship toward young people. Beautifully and honestly written, Sarah shares her parenting journey and offers a biblical, relevant, and clear 'discipleship GPS' that points to a healthy parenting eco-system. Sarah provides a real pathway focused on a foundational spiritual parenting practice while at the same time addressing the real-world issues that are faced by parents every day. Dig in deep—this book will change how you parent your children."

Tim Ciccone, director of youth ministry for the Evangelical Covenant Church

"Equipping parents to disciple their children may just be the most important thing we do to prepare the church for the next great move of God. This book is my first choice for that task. It thrills me to imagine how this book could equip a generation of families facing one of the most spiritually challenging periods in our country's history."

Ryan Pfeiffer, lead pastor of North Coast Calvary Chapel and coauthor with James Choung of *Longing for Revival: From Holy Discontent to Breakthrough Faith*

TEACH YOUR CHILDREN WELL

A
Step-by-Step
Guide for
Family
Discipleship

Sarah Cowan Johnson

An imprint of InterVarsity Press
Downers Grove, Illinois

InterVarsity Press
P.O. Box 1400 | Downers Grove, IL 60515-1426
ivpress.com | email@ivpress.com

InterVarsity Press® is the publishing division of InterVarsity Christian Fellowship/USA®. For more information, visit intervarsity.org.

All Scripture quotations, unless otherwise indicated, are taken from The Holy Bible, New International Version®, NIV®. Copyright © 1973, 1978, 1984, 2011 by Biblica, Inc.™ Used by permission of Zondervan. All rights reserved worldwide. www.zondervan.com. The "NIV" and "New International Version" are trademarks registered in the United States Patent and Trademark Office by Biblica, Inc.™

While any stories in this book are true, some names and identifying information may have been changed to protect the privacy of individuals.

Hand-drawn figures are by the author.

The publisher cannot verify the accuracy or functionality of website URLs used in this book beyond the date of publication.

Cover design and image composite: David Fassett

Interior design: Jeanna Wiggins

ISBN 978-1-5140-0380-0 (print) | ISBN 978-1-5140-0381-7 (digital)

Printed in the United States of America ∞

Library of Congress Cataloging-in-Publication Data
Names: Johnson, Sarah Cowan, 1981- author.
Title: Teach your children well : a step-by-step guide for family discipleship / Sarah Cowan Johnson.
Description: Downers Grove, IL : InterVarsity Press, [2022] | Includes bibliographical references.
Identifiers: LCCN 2022013854 (print) | LCCN 2022013855 (ebook) | ISBN 9781514003800 (print) |
    ISBN 9781514003817 (digital)
Subjects: LCSH: Christian education of children. | Parenting–Religious aspects–Christianity. |
    Child rearing–Religious aspects–Christianity.
Classification: LCC BV1475.3 .J64 2022 (print) | LCC BV1475.3 (ebook) | DDC 248.8/45–dc23/
    eng/20220622
LC record available at https://lccn.loc.gov/2022013854
LC ebook record available at https://lccn.loc.gov/2022013855

29   28   27   26   25   24   23 | 8   7   6   5   4

For Mom

I still want to be like you

when I grow up.

CONTENTS

INTRODUCTION

I LIVE IN PROVIDENCE, Rhode Island, with my husband and two boys. To get to our house from the highway, we usually take the Douglas Avenue exit, which takes us through Smith Hill into Elmhurst. It also takes us right past the Foxy Lady, an establishment that advertises its 6:00 a.m. "Legs and Eggs" breakfast on a billboard featuring not one but two pairs of sexy lady legs in enormous black heels.

I knew the question would come from the back seat one day: "Mom, what's the Foxy Lady?" I did not want to lie to them. I wanted them to hear about strip clubs from me before some kid with a phone showed them a video in the back of the school bus. To be honest, I wanted them to link the idea of the Foxy Lady to a distortion of God's view of women and their bodies, and I wanted that link to lodge viscerally in their developing brains. So I took a deep breath and did my best. I told them it was a place where men paid money for women to take their clothes off and that it was not a good place for women. They were appropriately horrified. One of them suggested we call the police. I told them it wasn't illegal (cue additional shock). I dismissed a few other suggestions involving guns and flamethrowers. In the end, I told them they could do what I do every time I drive by: pray that it will close.

Raising young Jesus-followers is not for the faint of heart. Helping to guide them into their own adult relationship with

Jesus is the greatest gift we can give them; at the end of our lives, and theirs, it's the thing that will matter most. But sometimes the journey there seems unclear to us or fraught with obstacles along the way, such as an unfortunately placed billboard.

But here's the thing: our life is full of opportunities to disciple our children. And, whether or not we disciple them, they *will* be discipled—by billboards, by kids in the back of the school bus, and by a world that does not know Jesus and his love.

Silas, who was six at the time, was paying close attention. The impact of this drive-by discipleship moment was so significant that a few days later our babysitter relayed the following conversation:

Silas: Do you know about the Foxy Lady?

Ashley: [Thinking he could not possibly mean *the* Foxy Lady and that this must be some kind of character from a show.] No, I don't think so . . .

Silas: Ashley, do *not* go there. There are men there who will try to pay you money to take your clothes off. Promise me you will never go there.

We were one part mortified, one part doubled over in laughter, and one part incredibly proud that in his six-year-old way, Silas was doing his best to love his babysitter.

This book is for parents, stepparents, foster parents, grandparents, aunties and uncles (genetic or spiritual), and all others who want to see our children—whether "ours" specifically or collectively—learn to walk the way of Jesus for the rest of their lives.

This book is for single parents juggling a thousand roles, married couples living at home with their children, blended families, "3G" families where grandparents play a large role in child-rearing, and for those FaceTiming in from thousands of miles away. It's for parents of newborns and teenagers, with an only child or whole soccer teams at their dining room tables.

This book is for those who have been loving and following Jesus for years and for those who are still discovering their own spiritual path.

This book is designed to help us lean into our calling as parents to guide our children into an adult relationship with Jesus.

HIGH GRACE, HIGH CHALLENGE

I am such a fan of these two-by-two, matrix-style grids that my friends joke I need to get a blank grid tattooed on my forearm. That way whenever a matrix would enhance a conversation, I would have easy access to one.

For this particular conversation, the values of Grace and Challenge will be essential to keep in our back pockets. Grace says, "Come just as you are and let God meet you wherever you're at." Challenge says, "We can't talk about something this critical without trying to do something about it." When these two values intersect, they form a grid with four quadrants, the Grace/Challenge Matrix.

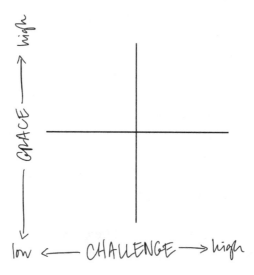

The lower left quadrant—Low Grace, Low Challenge—is what I call the Stagnation quadrant, a place of little to no growth. Without grace, this quadrant is cold and bleak, but without challenge, there's no incentive to leave it. These parents constantly feel like spiritual failures (spoiler alert: you are not a failure) but have little motivation to try something new.

The upper left quadrant—High Grace, Low Challenge—is what I call the All Set quadrant. On the surface, this quadrant looks cozy and warm. This is a quadrant of liberty, of acceptance, of welcome. We know we are loved, just as we are, no matter what we manage to accomplish as parents. But the dark underbelly of this quadrant is that, without challenge, it's just as motionless as the Stagnation quadrant. These parents take a hands-off approach to discipleship for the sake of freedom but often feel unsure how to engage when challenges arise.

The lower right quadrant, on the other hand—Low Grace, High Challenge—has the opposite problem. This is the quadrant of Shame. There's a lot of activity here. It's a quadrant of constant motion, ruthless evaluation, and endless striving. There's always more to be done and we never measure up to our own standards. These parents want to do everything right and carry the weight of their kids' spiritual futures on their shoulders.

What we're aiming for is the upper right quadrant—High Grace, High Challenge—the quadrant of Freedom. This is where real change is possible. In this quadrant we know that we are loved and accepted, just as we are. But we also feel an invitation to learn, grow, and experiment. We know that we will make mistakes as we help our kids follow Jesus, but we feel secure in our imperfections. In this environment, we and our children will thrive. These parents feel free to grow as disciples of Jesus, even as they disciple their own kids.

The path to Freedom will look different for each of us based on where we're starting from. If you aren't opposed to writing in books, put a little X on the grid where you naturally live. Then draw an arrow from that X into the Freedom quadrant. In the "Questions for Reflection" section at the end of this chapter, I'll give you some space to brainstorm specific ways you might encourage movement along this arrow, but here are a couple ideas to start you off:

- For those of us who live in the Stagnation quadrant, we will need to access more grace *and* more challenge for this journey. We'll need to remember that our relationship with Jesus is a free gift of grace, but we are invited, as Paul says in Philippians 3:16, to "live up to what we have already attained." This paradox may be challenging to embrace at first—we cannot earn this gift, but our effort matters—and we may find ourselves detouring through one of the other quadrants en route to the upper right. If that happens, please remember not to stay there! This Philippians passage may be a helpful one to spend some time with, considering what it means to "press on to take hold" (challenge) "of that for which Christ Jesus took hold of me" (grace)(v. 12).

- If we are operating from the All Set quadrant, we'll need to push ourselves (gently) to act and to engage. It may be helpful to acknowledge the painful or uncomfortable realities of family life that you'd like to see change, rather than continuing to sweep them under the rug. You could journal about them or even create something of a vision board for your family, motivating yourself with a concrete picture of the future you'd like to see realized. James 2:17 is a helpful corrective reminder that "faith by itself, if it is not accompanied by action, is dead."

- If we live in the Shame quadrant, our invitation is to remind ourselves that we are human. Sometimes—and counterintuitively—being incapable of receiving grace can actually be a symptom of pride. If you constantly struggle to feel good about yourself, find yourself being overly self-critical, and tend to beat yourself up for every little misstep and mistake, it may be an indication that you are using a measure that no human being except Jesus could ever live up to. The first step toward Freedom involves admitting that you are not, and will never be, perfect. And the second is recognizing that this fact does not make you less deserving of God's love and grace, but is the primary qualification for it. It may be helpful for you to reflect on 2 Corinthians 12:9-10 as you remember that God's power is made perfect in human weakness.

HOLY DISCONTENT

Buyer beware: there may be times when reading this book will highlight an area of deficit, a place where you see room for growth or improvement in your family's walk with Jesus. This isn't always comfortable. Recently, my husband, Greg, and I had a moment like this when our younger son, Silas, looked at us blankly when we assumed knowledge of a very common Bible story. He had no idea what we were talking about. We realized we hadn't spent nearly as much time reading the Bible with him as we had with our older son Noah when he was Si's age. It was an uncomfortable realization for us.

The quadrant you are operating from will determine how you respond to these moments. The response in the All Set quadrant is often an "Oh, well" kind of posture—hands thrown in the air with a laugh and a quick mental pivot to something more pleasant. "Haha whoops, guess we missed that one! #secondchild." The response in the Shame quadrant is to wallow in self-criticism and regret, which can lead to hopelessness and despair. "We are the worst parents, he's so behind, we have probably completely ruined his faith."

In the Freedom quadrant, however, we are able to experience something called holy discontent, which can lead us to a prayerful, hopeful longing. Holy discontent is a dissatisfaction with the status quo—a dissatisfaction we can be confident Jesus would share. When we allow it to, holy discontent will often lead us to a place of participation with God's Spirit to heal and restore whatever is broken. The invitation to participate is clear but not harsh. In this case, Greg and I felt convicted but not ashamed. It awakened a longing in us that Silas would grow in his knowledge and love of God's Word, and it lit a fire under us to spend more time reading with him. In the end, we felt truly thankful for the increased awareness and ready to make some changes.

A NOTE TO SINGLE PARENTS

You might find yourself on this journey alone. Perhaps your spouse, partner, or co-parent is not supportive of the steps you are taking with your children. Or perhaps, whether through death or a fractured relationship, a second parent is simply not in the picture at all. This is one of the most profoundly challenging places to start from, and you face unique demands. I acknowledge this, and I see you. And I am confident God will meet you right in the middle of your reality—both because I believe this is simply what God does and because I've seen it with my own two eyes. My friend Sarah is a single mom to two children, ages eleven and fourteen. She participated in my six-week Parents Cohort[1] and sent me this note afterward:

> During this process I learned to surrender to God as "co-parent" to my kids. I was sort of envious of people with spouses when we began, but through this process God showed up, and I was shown that he was all that I needed.

She went on to describe a very specific way that she needed God to "back her up" as her only partner in this parenting journey—and God pulled through in a miraculous way that can only be described as an answer to prayer. She said this:

I felt honored that God came through and I continue to be intimate with him, asking for the weirdest things and support. I'm actually thankful to be alone because I have to rely fully on Jesus. We all do, but being single gives us that extra opportunity to be without.

You may not be at the point where you are ready or able to use the word *thankful* the way Sarah does here, but I hope that you'll come to experience God the way Sarah has, as your co-parent, your partner, and the one who has your back.

QUESTIONS FOR REFLECTION

1. Why did you decide to read this book and what are you hoping to gain?

2. What specific questions are you bringing into this conversation?

3. Return to the Grace/Challenge Matrix for a moment. When it comes to discipling your kids, which quadrant do you gravitate toward most naturally? What will it take to move in the direction of the arrow you drew? What will you need to remind yourself? What Scriptures, rhythms, or practices could help you here?

4. What do you need from Jesus today?

For pastors and church leaders

1. What motivates you the most about partnering with parents and equipping them to disciple their children?

2. Which quadrant best describes your church culture? What steps could you take to help parents in your community live from the Freedom quadrant?

1

THE BAD NEWS

(or A Street Atlas and an Ashtray Full of Quarters)

If there's a 50/50 chance that something can go wrong, then 9 times out of 10 it will.

PAUL HARVEY

S O HERE'S THE THING, FRIENDS: I have bad news, and I have good news. I'm going to start with the bad news because, even if it lands like a punch in the gut, the anticipation of some good news will hopefully soften the blow.

At this moment in the United States, the odds of our children walking with Jesus as adults are equivalent to that of a coin toss. The Fuller Youth Institute estimates that 50 percent of high school students actively involved in their churches walk away from their faith after graduation.[1] Pay attention to that phrasing: It's not 50 percent of churched high school students or those who attend church occasionally. It's 50 percent of teens who are actively involved in their churches. We are talking about 50 percent of our most committed youth groupers choosing to do life apart from Jesus as adults.

I don't know about you, but this does not sit well with me—at all. I feel it in my gut every time I think about it, a churning discomfort that grows into a raging fire within me to *do* something. Not just for my own two boys but for a generation of young people and for the sake of humanity's continued relationship with God. I am unwilling to entrust my children's future relationship with Jesus to a coin toss. And I firmly believe that we absolutely do not have to.

As parents, much to our frustration and emotional turmoil, it's important to remember that we cannot ever guarantee—no matter how faithfully we engage their spiritual journey and how hard we pray for them—that our children will follow Jesus as adults. As Greg liked to remind me when our infants simply would not sleep no matter how many sleep strategies we tried, they are not robots. They cannot be programmed to do what we want them to.

And so I'm not saying there is some magic formula that, by our own effort, will produce perfect little ~~robots~~ disciples. As enchanting as that idea might be to those of us who would prefer to be in control of all things at all times, it is simply unrealistic. It's also theologically bankrupt. Scripture is clear that a relationship with Jesus is initiated by God (John 6:44) and the part we play is simply opening the door to God's knock (Revelation 3:20). As parents, while we can do everything in our power to amplify the knocking, we cannot force our children to open that door. To believe anything different is to assume a place in our children's lives that rightfully belongs to God (idolatry) or to them (enmeshment).

This misconception can lead to shame, which is never from the Lord. If you are the parent of a child who has walked away from Jesus, your heartache reflects the heart of God. But if you carry any sense of shame or failure, please hear my invitation to lay those burdens at the feet of Jesus. The enemy would love to discourage you—or even deter you from continuing to pray for your child—by lying to you and heaping an undue burden on your shoulders. It may be helpful to remember that your children have always been a trust: they belong to God, not to you. You are not responsible for, or capable of, determining the outcome of their journey. God knows and loves your children more than you will ever comprehend. And as the story of the prodigal son(s) in Luke 15 demonstrates, no one is ever beyond the scope of God's reach and grace.

So as long as we are clear on this from the beginning—that there are no guarantees, even if we do everything "right"—I think there's a whole lot we can explore that will equip us to lead our children to a maturing faith and leave that 50 percent statistic in the dust.

HOW DID WE GET HERE?

I grew up in the eighties. I watched the Challenger explode and the Berlin Wall come down. I had a pink banana-seat Huffy bike with streamers on the handlebars. I died of dysentery hundreds of times on the Oregon Trail, and I remember when skinny jeans went out of style the first time. I also remember what it was like to learn to drive without a GPS.

Spatial intelligence and an intuitive sense of direction are two things that the Lord did not bless me with—and that's putting it mildly. When I got my driver's license, my dad joked that he wished he could buy me a homing pigeon to take with me in the car. (When I was twenty-four, and TomTom made the first all-in-one personal navigation GPS device, Dad sent me one in the mail with a note that said, "Finally: your homing pigeon.") Whenever I drove anywhere alone, I planned extra time for getting lost. My Massachusetts Street Atlas was my best friend. And I always kept quarters in my car's ashtray (yes, you read that correctly, younger readers: ashtray) for payphone calls.

For me, getting lost was a normal part of driving. The first step to finding my way again was figuring out where I was. First, I'd need to figure out what town I was in, then locate two cross streets and look them up in the atlas. At that point, I would try to retrace my steps—"How did I get here?"—to find my way back to my ill-fated wrong turn.

As I think about where we are when it comes to helping our kids walk the way of Jesus, that 50 percent statistic indicates that we in the Western church are lost. For those who remember pre-GPS driving, it's the moment when what you are seeing out your window doesn't match where you expected to find yourself. We are lost. And to find our way again, it's helpful to first retrace our steps—to ask, "How did we get here?"—so that we identify the wrong turns we've made along the way.

To be honest, there are probably too many wrong turns to count, but I'm going to explore a few, loosely labeled under the subheadings of the world, the church, and us.

THE WORLD

The world around us is changing and has changed significantly in the last twenty years. If you are my age or older, you have lived through this shift as an adult and may be acutely aware of the sea change, though you may not be able to put your finger on exactly what it is or why it's happening. Maybe you don't understand why everyone younger than you lists their pronouns everywhere. If you are a decade or more younger than me, you have likely come of age amid this shift and may not even be aware of it. Pronouns are a completely normal part of life.

Prior to the turn of the twenty-first century, with respect to Christianity, there were only two types of cultures in the world: what we might call "non-Christian" cultures (societies with no historic Christian influence) and those we could call "Christendom" (societies where Christianity had exerted strong cultural influence). But for the first time in human history, the twenty-first century has brought about the emergence of a third type of culture in Western societies, what scholars refer to as "post-Christian culture."[2]

Now, I am writing this from Providence, Rhode Island—recently ranked by the Barna Group as the third most post-Christian city in the United States.[3] If you are reading this from the Bible Belt, you may feel like I'm talking about another planet as your context may still feel more like Christendom. But if you haven't yet experienced this shift, know that it's absolutely coming your way.

Post-Christian culture is unique because it is a reaction to Christianity. It is familiar with Christianity but has rejected it. Most vaccines work by exposing the human body to enough of a virus—a weakened version of it—to enable the immune system to defend itself against it. This is called *inoculation*. In the same way, post-Christian cultures have been exposed to enough of the gospel—a weakened version of it, usually—to become inoculated to it.

Some distinctives of a post-Christian culture include (1) a particular adeptness in deconstructing the Christian worldview; (2) an interest in the values of the kingdom (e.g., justice, the dignity of all human beings, etc.) without the authority of the King; (3) a sense that the moral high ground has shifted from the religious sector to the secular sector (for example, the Christian sexual ethic used to be seen as peculiar, perhaps, but a generally moral way to live); and (4) an almost pharisaical judgmentalism toward the way of Jesus when it cuts against the grain of mainstream culture.

For our discussion, this means that our children are growing up in a world that is discipling them in these post-Christian distinctives. When I was in high school, those who knew my (traditional) views on sex often told me, "Oh you're such a good person, Sarah." This head-patting sometimes embarrassed me, but there was a baseline level of respect in the air for my choices. Today, that same ethic is very often viewed as immoral, repressive, and even harmful. I'm quite confident my kids will not receive the same kudos for the choices they (hopefully) make about their bodies.

Though many of us have become decidedly used to it, myself included, it's important to remember that post-Christian culture is not neutral to the way of Jesus. It is actually quite hostile to it. Now, I'm not saying that Christendom was any better. You will not hear me longing for the "glory days" of the last century, because Christendom came with its own very real threats to the way of Jesus. Christianity and Christendom are not interchangeable terms; one is about walking the way of Jesus, the other is about cultural power and privilege (two things Jesus didn't actually have).

Honestly, I'm not convinced that this shift is fundamentally bad for the future of Christianity, in the same way that living in exile wasn't fundamentally bad for Israel, and persecution wasn't fundamentally bad for the growth of the early church or the modern Chinese church. The people of God adapted in these scenarios and allowed the trials and tribulations of these moments to cause them to depend on God's power rather than their own. Pining to return to Christendom, where there was cultural power, is not unlike the Israelites pining to return to Egypt where there was meat.

So please do not hear me longing to reclaim the cultural power and privilege Christians once had. But, we must not forget that the world around us, apart from Jesus, is lost. If you're like me, you may be tempted to try to view these post-Christian distinctives as little more than "alternative paths through life." I don't particularly like calling them "wrong turns," because I don't particularly like feeling like a caricature of the judgmental zealot the world expects me to be as a Jesus-follower. But these paths do not lead us anywhere we truly want to go. They, along with several other twists and turns, have led us to a land we don't recognize, where 50 percent of our children are leaving the faith as adults.

THE CHURCH

Have your kids ever had a fight where what distressed you more than the original infraction was the way they treated each other during the fight? That's how I feel about post-Christian culture and the church. What concerns me even more than the fact that our kids are being discipled by the values of a post-Christian world is how the Western church has, by and large, responded to this fact.

When animals are threatened, they tend to respond with one of three primary responses: fight, flight, or camouflage. Bears will try to maul you, deer quite literally hightail it, and chameleons try their hardest to look just like the rock they're sitting on. In many ways, this is how the Western church has responded to the cultural shifts of the twenty-first century:

- Fight: These are the culture-war churches, who have tried to hold onto the trimmings and trappings of Christendom's declining cultural power by fixating on political candidates and court battles.

- Flight: These are the foxhole churches, who have evacuated mainstream culture in favor of monocultural Christian environments.

- Camouflage: These are the syncretistic churches, who have sought to blend into the shifting culture and have adopted many of the values, attitudes, and even theological perspectives of the post-Christian milieu.

These responses are nothing new. In Jesus' day, the Jewish community responded in much the same way to Roman occupation. The Zealots chose to fight, quite literally attempting to overthrow Rome by force. The Essenes, and to some extent the Pharisees, went the flight route, separating themselves off completely from anything that might defile them. And the Sadducees chose the camouflage option, rejecting the oral tradition of their ancestors and accommodating as needed to survive.

If the 50 percent statistic is evidence that we are lost, then each of these responses has been a wrong turn somewhere along the way—because none of these responses are helping our children to walk the way of Jesus confidently in a world that doesn't. Children raised to "fight" will expect, and find, battles everywhere. Children raised to "flee" will struggle to translate their experience of God into a secular setting. And children raised to "camouflage" will fear critique and criticism by their peers—of which there will be plenty—more than anything else. We need to recalculate and find a new route forward.

But before we do that, there are a couple of other wrong turns in the church category that deserve an honorable mention.

The professionalization of the priesthood. One of the primary doctrines of the Protestant Reformation of the sixteenth century was "the priesthood of all believers." The leaders of this movement, seeking the reform of the state church, felt strongly about liberating the work of ministry from a small elite class of priests and inviting every Christian to join God in the work of renewal in their daily lives. But, five hundred years later, many churches who trace their spiritual heritage back to this movement don't actually seem to embody this doctrine in practice. Our church, Sanctuary Church in Providence, uses the analogy of a football field. In many churches today, the church staff appear to be the only ones on the field. They are the ones faithfully doing the work of kingdom ministry while the congregation watches from the stands, cheering them on (or, all too often, booing and complaining loudly about how they could improve their game). Sanctuary hopes that our church staff will operate more like the coaches and trainers and medics—and even cheerleaders—with the congregation out on the field, partnering with Jesus in the work he's called them to do in their own contexts: at work, in their neighborhoods, and in their homes. As Aaron Niequist puts it, "[Church staff] have a role to play, to be sure, but their primary job is to launch everyone else into the remaining 166 hours of the week."[4]

Parents are one group that too many churches have kept in the stands for far too long. While helicopter parenting and the tendency to be over-involved is a real dynamic for some, when it comes to discipleship, many of us sit in the bleachers week in and week out. We watch the youth pastors and children's ministry directors and Sunday school teachers run plays, feeling relieved that folks with experience are wearing our colors. And all the while nobody realizes, least of all parents, that we would very likely become the MVPs if we were handed the ball. One critical way for the church to find our way again is to revisit the doctrine of the priesthood of all believers, equipping and empowering every follower of Jesus to find their place in God's mission.

Mass-marketed Sunday school curricula. I remember four-year-old Noah coming home from Sunday school one week with one of those little parent handouts summarizing the day's lesson (you know, the ones that typically make their way directly to the recycling bin without so much as a glance). The lesson that day was about Noah, his favorite character in the Bible for obvious reasons. The lesson's key takeaway was, "Noah was kind to the animals. How can you be kind to your family this week?" I was taken aback. How could the story of Noah—a story about hearing God's voice and obeying when everyone else thinks you're crazy, about judgment and rescue, about God's redemption of humanity—*how* could this story become diluted to the point that we are discussing saccharine takeaways about being nice to animals?

Well, let me tell you exactly how this could be.

Prior to the late nineteenth century, the primary tool for religious education was a catechism, a summary of the basic tenets of the Christian faith in the form of questions and answers. This tool, used with both children and new believers, taught the larger picture of the story of God. It covered topics such as creation and the fall of humanity, the nature of the Trinity, the pathway to salvation, the purpose of the church, and the future return of Jesus. For example, here is an excerpt from the well-known Westminster Catechism:

Q1. What is man's primary purpose?

Man's primary purpose is to glorify God, and to enjoy him forever.

Q2. What authority from God directs us how to glorify and enjoy Him?

The only authority for glorifying and enjoying Him is the Bible, which is the Word of God and is made up of the Old and New Testaments.

Q3. What does the Bible primarily teach?

The Bible primarily teaches what man must believe about God and what God requires of man.

Q4. What is God?

God is a spirit, Whose being, wisdom, power, holiness, justice, goodness, and truth are infinite, eternal, and unchangeable.[5]

Near the end of the nineteenth century and throughout the first part of the twentieth century, several waves of revival swept through Europe and the United States, dramatically increasing the numbers of new believers in need of religious instruction. To meet this demand, lay people began to join the ranks of religious educators, previously limited to clergy. This was the beginning of what became known as the Sunday School Movement. On the surface, this was a wonderful thing as hundreds of lay people across the Western world were empowered to partner with clergy in response to a move of God's Spirit.

But how do you train and equip a whole new class of religious educators with no access to seminaries? Before long, parachurch ministries called Sunday School Guilds began to form. Their mission was to resource and equip these lay teachers with curricula and training. Because they were parachurch ministries, they were interdenominational. And because they were interdenominational, they didn't always agree on the finer points of doctrine contained in the various catechisms used by the major denominations. So these Sunday School Guilds made the decision, due to their interdenominational audience, to base their curricula solely on the one teaching tool that every major denomination could agree on: the Bible.

On face value, this sounds amazing. Denominations working together, empowering lay people, and depending on the Bible as the baseline for religious instruction. But as J. I. Packer and Gary Parrett discuss in their book *Grounded in the Gospel*,

> But is it really possible to avoid teaching doctrinal controversy by teaching the Bible? In order to come as close as possible to achieving this goal, it was inevitable that the focus of the biblical teaching would shift from doctrinal emphasis and would arrive at last at the teaching of Bible stories. While the teaching of Bible stories is surely a good thing, this has often been done in a way that separates the particular stories from the broader story of God's redemptive dealings with humankind. This in turn can easily mean that attention is taken away from the grace of God revealed in Jesus Christ to mere rehearsal of episodic events, often followed by moral admonition: "We see Jonah got himself in trouble, so we had better not . . ." "Mary gave herself wholly to the Lord, and so should we." A child who has grown up even recently in an evangelical Sunday school will likely be very familiar with the stories of Noah, Moses, Jonah, and Mary. But that same child will be far less

likely to be able to recite the Apostles' Creed or enumerate the Ten Commandments.[6]

Fast forward a couple hundred years, throw in market pressures and profit margins, and this is how the story of Noah turned into a conversation about being nice. Now, you might be thinking, "Your son was only four! Did you really expect his Sunday school teachers to talk to him about hearing God's voice? Or about the wrath of God?" To be completely frank, yes.

Here's what troubles me deeply about this trend: the Sticky Faith researchers at the Fuller Youth Institute suggest that a robust understanding of the gospel is one of the key factors in developing a faith that "sticks" from childhood into adulthood.[7] The same study also found that a primary confusion among teenagers about the gospel is around the role of behavior. "Many young people see faith like a jacket: something they can put on or take off based on their behavior."[8] Is it any wonder that our kids are confused about the role of behavior when we haven't helped them, for example, connect the Noah story to the larger story of God's grace and rescue, and we instead have encouraged them to focus only on Noah's good behavior?

In short, this is a massive wrong turn, like full north instead of south on the highway. As we eventually find our way again, a significant consideration should be helping our kids understand the larger narrative arc of Scripture and their place in God's eternal purposes.

US

Finally, we parents have taken a few wrong turns as well. And, when I say that, I don't mean the missteps and mistakes we've each made personally on this journey. That is unavoidable; we are human beings who are both sinful and fallible. (By the way, if your kids do not know these two facts about you, please tell them now. Talk about this often. Apologize to your kids and ask for their forgiveness whenever you are wrong. You would be surprised how many children grow up assuming their parents are neither sinful nor fallible and are deeply disillusioned later in life when they learn the truth in a more dramatic way.) What I mean is the wrong turns we've taken collectively as parents. And this one rises to the top: in nearly every area of life, when we want our children to grow or succeed at something, we hand them over to the professionals. We hire math tutors and soccer coaches and sign them up for voice lessons. This is completely normal in our society and makes a lot of sense. We hired music teachers for our kids (piano and drums) as soon as their skills eclipsed our own.

Our wrong turn has been assuming that this otherwise very sensible logic applies to our kids' spiritual development. When the church provides us with a children's pastor or youth pastor—or even Sunday school teacher—we breathe a sigh of relief and hand our children over to the ones who are "paid the big bucks" and, we assume, are much more qualified than we are to train our children in this area. (Note how our preference for professional teachers and trainers pairs very nicely with the church's emphasis on professional ministers.)

The only problem is that this logic doesn't apply to our children's spiritual development. Now, please don't get me wrong. Paid children, youth, and family ministers are an incredible gift to the church and an important piece of the puzzle when it comes to children's faith development. But they are not an adequate replacement for the spiritual leadership of the parent. The data is clear on this: the leadership of parents is essential when it comes to helping children learn to walk the way of Jesus.

In my pre-GPS life, one of the worst parts of getting lost was the initial sense of impending doom as I began to realize I was not on the right track, followed by the utter confusion of driving around in circles trying to find my way back to something I recognized—a landmark, a street sign, anything. So there was always a certain sense of relief in finally deciding to pull into a gas station and admit I was lost, because that was the first step in finding my way again.

I'm hoping that you are feeling that sense of relief right now. The truth is we didn't mean to end up here, with 50 percent of our kids walking away from Jesus as adults. So it's okay—and perhaps even liberating—to admit that we are lost and we need a little help getting back on the right path.

QUESTIONS FOR REFLECTION

1. How does the 50 percent statistic make you feel? What thoughts or emotions come up as you reflect on it?

2. What has your experience of post-Christian culture been like? Has it felt more like a crosscultural experience or more like your cultural "home"? When it comes to helping your children learn to follow Jesus in a post-Christian world, what are the implications of your answer?

3. Of the three responses to post-Christian culture—fight, flight, or camouflage—do you resonate with any of them? Which one are you most tempted to emulate? How might your particular posture affect your kids' views of the world?

4. On a scale of one to five, how strongly do you resonate with the idea that church leaders and staff seem better equipped to disciple your children than you are?

For pastors and church leaders

1. Which of the three responses to post-Christian culture is your church most likely to gravitate toward? Is this the same or different from your natural response?

2. How does the organization and structure of your church reflect the idea of the priesthood of all believers? Who is running the plays on the field? Who is in the stands?

3. How are children in your church community learning about the larger story of God and their place in that story? Does your Sunday school curriculum help children to understand the gospel of grace or the gospel of good behavior?

2

A LITTLE YEAST

> *The most eloquent testimony to the reality*
> *of the resurrection is not an empty tomb or a*
> *well-orchestrated pageant on Easter Sunday*
> *but rather a group of people whose life together*
> *is so radically different, so completely changed*
> *from the way the world builds a community, that*
> *there can be no explanation other than that*
> *something decisive has happened in history.*
>
> **WILL WILLIMON, *ACTS: INTERPRETATION***

THE GOOD NEWS IS COMING SOON. I promise. But first we need to understand why this conversation matters so much—not just on a personal level, but on a global one.

In Matthew 13:33, Jesus tells this parable: "The kingdom of heaven is like yeast that a woman took and mixed into about sixty pounds of flour until it worked all through the dough." Think about it: sixty pounds of flour (the equivalent of my eight-year-old) is a heavy lift for that yeast. It's a ridiculous amount of flour for one woman to be kneading by herself—enough to bake five dozen loaves. Jesus is being hyperbolic to illustrate the potentially massive effect even a little yeast can have on its environment.

In a similar way, discipling your children may seem like a minuscule corrective in the grand scheme of where we've gone wrong in the Western church. In the face of all we've just discussed, how can we ever hope to make a difference? But just like a little yeast can affect a much larger quantity of flour, I believe helping our kids walk the way of Jesus today will affect not just their lives, but humanity's ongoing relationship with God. Let me explain.

ACTIVATE THE PARENTS

The connection between families and God's wider purposes in the world is nothing new. Parents have always been part of God's redemptive plan for humanity. This is not to say that parents have been more significant to God's plan than married people without children, single people without children, or those who have longed to become parents but haven't been able to. In fact, those without children often contribute to God's mission in ways that parents simply can't (1 Corinthians 7:6-8). But from the first parents, who were given a mandate to fill the world with God's image through their procreation, to Jesus himself being entrusted to human parents to raise him, it's clear God has trusted human parents to share in his work and mission in significant ways.

We see this trust most clearly demonstrated in Deuteronomy 6. The Israelites have been wandering in the wilderness for nearly forty years, and finally—finally!—they are ready to enter the Promised Land. In the wilderness, despite its challenges (and their bitter disdain for it), they learned to be utterly dependent on God. God fed them with manna and quail; provided water for them from rocks; and showed them where to go with pillars of fire and smoke. They learned to walk in intimacy and dependence on God. And they did this in a monocultural context which provided no external threats to their relationship with Yahweh. The Promised Land, the land "flowing with milk and honey," and also full of polytheistic (idolatrous) cultures, will be different.

Moses, speaking to the people, says this in Deuteronomy 6:10-12:

> When the LORD your God brings you into the land he swore
> to your fathers, to Abraham, Isaac and Jacob, to give you—a
> land with large, flourishing cities you did not build, houses
> filled with all kinds of good things you did not provide, wells
> you did not dig, and vineyards and olive groves you did not
> plant—then when you eat and are satisfied, be careful that
> you do not forget the LORD, who brought you out of Egypt,
> out of the land of slavery.

The danger of no longer being dependent on manna and quail for
food, on fire and smoke for direction, on water miraculously
springing from rocks—the danger of living in a land of abundance,
surrounded by people who don't know Yahweh—is that Israel will
forget God. And if Israel forgets God, how will humanity continue
to know God? The stakes are incredibly high. Humanity's ongoing
relationship with God lies in the balance.

So what does God do? He instructs Moses to tell the people this:

> Hear, O Israel: The LORD our God, the LORD is one. Love the
> LORD your God with all your heart and with all your soul and
> with all your strength. These commandments that I give you
> today are to be on your hearts. Impress them on your
> children. Talk about them when you sit at home and when
> you walk along the road, when you lie down and when you
> get up. Tie them as symbols on your hands and bind them
> on your foreheads. Write them on the doorframes of your
> houses and on your gates. (Deuteronomy 6:4-9)

Facing the possibility that Israel—and all of humanity—will forget
God, what is God's strategy? "Activate the parents!" The critical
work of embedding his Word, which reveals his character and his
nature, in the hearts of his people— God entrusts this task not just
to prophets and priests, but to parents and children.

The instructions given to the Israelites are not to ensure that their children are formally educated by religious "professionals," but instead to repurpose life's ordinary moments for discipleship: sitting at home, walking along the road, and daily rhythms like bedtime and morning routines. Moses could have instructed the Israelites to set up schools to train children in the Scriptures. Deuteronomy 6:6-9 could have read more like this:

> These commandments that I give you today are to be on your hearts. Impress them on your children. Select from among the tribe of Levi forty men of noble character, who fear the Lord and love his statutes. Until the day the Lord your God brings you into the land he swore to your fathers, to Abraham, Isaac, and Jacob, to give you, these men shall be set apart to train your children. They shall set up schools that meet by day, and schools that meet by night, so that all your children will love the Lord your God and carry his commandments in their hearts. Then when you set your feet in the land the Lord your God swore to give you, you and your children will not forget the Lord, who brought you out of Egypt, out of the land of slavery.

Not the actual Bible.

That's not a terrible plan—but it's not the one God chooses. Instead, God chooses ordinary parents, like you and me, to repurpose ordinary moments to help our children learn to love and obey God. If Moses were giving these instructions to twenty-first-century parents, it might sound something like this:

> These commandments that I give you today are to be on your hearts. Impress them on your children. Talk about them at the dinner table, and as you walk to the bus stop, and as you drive to soccer practice, and as you shuttle them to and fro. Weave them into your bedtime routines, into bathtime and storytime, and when they ask for one last hug or a glass of water. Talk about them as you dress

your toddlers in the morning, as you pack school lunches for your tweens, and as you send your teenagers out the door for the day.

This was God's plan to ensure that Israel wouldn't forget God: he activated parents to repurpose everyday moments to help their children learn to love and follow God. And I can't think of a better strategy today. We are in a unique moment as a society. In recent years, we've experienced a global pandemic, polarizing politics, heightened awareness of racial injustice, and a war in Eastern Europe with massive geopolitical ramifications. The fabric of our society is, if not fraying outright, significantly strained. Simultaneously, the church is learning to navigate life and ministry in a novel post-Christian context. In many ways, we in the West are also in danger of forgetting God. Raising up the next generation to love, know, and follow God is just as essential now as it was in Moses' time.

This has significant implications for parents. Discipling our kids in this cultural moment requires us to accept the reality that, if we are successful, our kids will be misunderstood by the world around them. For those of us with crippling memories of childhood rejection, and even bullying, this may be terrifying. I was mocked in seventh grade for my short haircut, and I'm not sure I've ever fully recovered. It's hard for me to imagine my sweet, earnest boys being mocked by their peers for what they believe, and I'd do almost anything to protect them from that. The temptation to help them camouflage will be strong.

To walk the way of Jesus confidently in this moment, our kids—and we—will need more than just knowledge about God. They'll even need more than a strong personal relationship with Jesus. They'll need their head knowledge of God and heart intimacy with Jesus to form them into people who aren't afraid to *live* differently, peculiarly even.

And this kind of formation is not something that can be done in one hour of church programming on Sunday mornings. The kind of preparation our kids will need to live an alternative way of life—to walk the way of Jesus in a world that doesn't—will require God's age-old strategy: "Activate the parents!"

BECOMING A CREATIVE MINORITY

But how? How do we help our children to be faithful to God's kingdom, especially if it means being at odds with the world around them? In their essay titled "A Creative Minority," Jon Tyson and Heather Grizzle say this: "We need a vision that is not based on a fear of a godless future, or a longing for an idealized past, but a rich presence in our own time that inspires the beauty and possibility of Christ's church."[1] They put forth the vision of a creative minority, a Christian community that "seeks to function in a dominant culture for the purpose of being a redeeming factor within it."[2]

This concept is nothing new. Daniel and his friends in exile in Babylon are a perfect example of a creative minority. While they refused to participate in practices that would dishonor God—eating food sacrificed to idols, bowing down to a golden idol—they also remained committed to the flourishing of Babylon in such a way that they rose to positions of great influence and were used by God for his purposes. So this is not a brand-new idea. What's new is the Western church learning to identify with this experience after enjoying centuries of societal power and influence in the context of Christendom. Churches that became dependent on cultural power, perhaps more so than God's power, now feel threatened as they feel their influence waning. So instead of responding like Daniel—faithful to God, invested in society—they are more likely to respond with "fight, flight, or camouflage."

It strikes me that this little phrase—"function in a dominant culture for the purpose of being a redeeming factor within it"—contains a corrective for each of the three defensive postures of the Western church. Consider this chart:

RESPONSE	FIGHT	CAMOUFLAGE	FLIGHT
RATIONALE	win	survive	avoid
CORRECTIVE	Function in a dominant culture	for the purpose of being a redeeming factor	within it.
INVITATION	love and serve	lead and influence	commit

In the top row, you'll find the defensive posture we are trying to avoid. In the second row, you'll see the rationale for that posture. "Fight" churches want to win the war with the culture. "Camouflage" churches want to survive within the culture. And "Flight" churches want to avoid the culture. You'll then see how each posture finds a corrective within this definition of a creative minority and a corresponding invitation.

Fight. The corrective for the instinct to fight is to function in a dominant culture, and the invitation is to love and serve. Jeremiah 29:7, written to the exiles in Babylon, instructed them to "Seek the peace and prosperity of the city to which I have carried you into exile. Pray to the LORD for it, because if it prospers, you too will prosper." This is what Daniel did. Though he remained faithful to God by refusing to participate in cultural practices that would dishonor God, Daniel didn't stage a coup or try to defeat Babylon from within. Instead he functioned—even thrived— within Babylon, rising to become a trusted royal official.

If you lean more toward Fight by nature, you may resonate with attempts to regain Christianity's cachet through politics, protest, or legislation. The invitation for you is to look to Jesus, who gave up his divine prerogatives and privilege, and who revealed God's sacrificial enemy-love on the cross (Philippians 2:5-8). Rather than unleash his wrath on a broken world, God chose to enter it in love. The incarnation is our antidote to the Fight response: What could be less aggressive and threatening than a human baby? What would it look like for you to love and serve the "thems" of your world—to function and even thrive in this new context—rather than simply trying to win?

Camouflage. The corrective for the instinct to blend in and survive is to embrace the purpose of being a redeeming factor within that culture. I have talked to my boys many times about the kind of friendships they are developing. Occasionally I hear them talk about friends whose behavior is . . . less than savory. While some parents might try to restrict access to these friends, the conversation I prefer to have with my boys is about influence: Which direction is the influence flowing? If these friends are influencing you and their behavior is rubbing off on you, that's a very different scenario than if you are able to influence them. Even within their elementary and middle school social circles I want them to understand that they have a calling and a purpose to be a redeeming influence. The same principle applies to Jesus-followers living in a post-Christian world. The invitation, then, is to influence and to lead—to partner with God in his redemptive purposes.

Flight. The corrective for the Flight response is to function as a redeeming factor *within* the dominant culture. Removing ourselves and our families from secular culture does have some benefits when it comes to creating an environment conducive to the kind of formation this moment in history calls for. But there are two problems with this approach: One, unless we can guarantee that our kids will never reenter the post-Christian world, we do them no favors by omitting from their discipleship any modeling and practice around how to live differently from the world around them. And two, it is far too easy to neglect our missional call to demonstrate and proclaim the good news of Jesus when we don't rub shoulders with anyone who doesn't already know him. The invitation here is to commit to our neighborhoods, our cities, our workplaces, our kids' schools—everywhere we have been placed by God, like Daniel in Babylon, to be a redeeming influence.

PREPARING A REMNANT

Imagine a generation of young people who have learned to walk the way of Jesus confidently in a world that misunderstands them. Think about the impact these people could have on the church and on the world around them. Could it be possible that God is activating us to prepare our children for a unique role in his broader redemptive purposes?

From the very beginning of God's relationship with humanity, there has been an up-and-down ribbon running through the story line like a wave pattern.

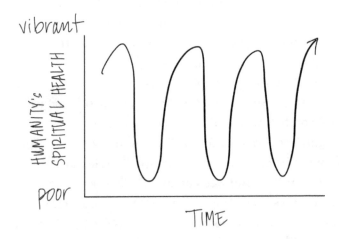

On the mountaintops, humanity is walking with God. In the valleys, they have forgotten him. And in every valley, eventually, God intervenes, pouring out his Spirit, renewing his people so that God's relationship with humanity does not continue to decline into nonexistence. We call this intervention and renewal "revival"—times of widespread spiritual awakening, large numbers of people coming to faith, and renewal within the church. In this country, we can point to the First and Second Great Awakenings of the eighteenth and nineteenth centuries, the Azusa Street Revival of the early twentieth century, and even the civil rights movement of the mid-twentieth century as examples of revival. But this pattern is not just a modern phenomenon. This up-and-down ribbon can be traced back through the centuries, even through Israel's story in the Old Testament. The pattern is consistent. When humanity strays too far—when we become too lost—God intervenes and brings us back home.[3]

When we look at the world around us, it seems likely that we in the West are, again, nearing a low point on the spiritual curve. The church in the West has been in decline for decades. Many historic churches are dying. This is not to say that there aren't vibrant expressions of the kingdom to be found, but that the world around us, by and large, has forgotten God and gotten lost. And the church, in its own strength, has struggled to provide the kind of renewal the world needs. Think again about the three responses of the Western church in this moment: fight, flight, camouflage. None of these are sufficient to bring about the kind of change we long to see in our world. None of these are sufficient to heal the cataclysmic racial, ethnic, and political divisions that have been so painfully exposed in our society. None of these are sufficient to bring about the healing, and justice, and freedom, and salvation we know our broken world so desperately needs.

Only God's intervention, an outpouring of his Spirit—only revival—can do this. And, historically, when God does this, he first empowers a remnant to receive and steward this work of the Spirit and to lead humanity back into harmony with him. From Elijah at Carmel, to Nehemiah, to the disciples of John the

Baptist, to the Franciscans in pre-Renaissance Europe, to the Pietists in Moravia, to the Black church in the Jim Crow South. In moments of widespread spiritual decline, God has always looked for those who are faithful to his kingdom—and often at odds with the culture around them—to serve as leaders and shepherds of his people when he intervenes.

As we prepare our children to confidently walk the way of Jesus in a world that doesn't know him, there's a growing sense in my spirit that you and I and our children just might be the remnant God is preparing to steward a massive work of his Spirit in our midst.

PLAYING OUR PART

If all this big-picture discussion feels overwhelming, think of an orchestra playing a beautiful piece of music. There is no way that one musician could sit down and play a symphony alone; if you were to isolate the viola part, it would probably sound relatively simple. Each musician is only responsible for his or her part. But as they tune to the concertmaster's pitch and follow the conductor's lead, they become wrapped up into something much larger and more beautiful than themselves.

The same goes for you: to be part of this larger story, all you have to do is play your specific part. Your friends, your church community, perhaps your parents or other family members will have a part to play as well. And your children also have their own parts. You are not responsible for creating the symphony—that is the conductor's responsibility. You are simply invited to play your part.

One idea that I invite you to carry with you on this journey is a classic leadership principle by Stephen Covey: the healthiest people focus their energy and effort on the (smaller) Circle of Influence within their (infinite) Circle of Concern.[4]

As parents, we are concerned about endless lists of things. From the moment our babies begin to walk, the world comes at them

fast, and there is so much we can worry
about! From blankets in cribs to
uncut grapes to growth curves to
school decisions to bullies and
heartache and driving while
texting and colleges and . . .
Our Circle of Concern is so
endless we might even call it
the Black Hole of Concern. We
can spend all our mental energy
there, which Covey says will lead to
reactivity, or we can focus our attention
on the few things within our Circle of Influence, the specific part
God has invited us to play, which Covey says will lead to proactivity.

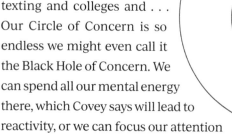

When it comes to helping your children learn to walk the way
of Jesus, it will be essential for you to identify what's in your
Circle of Influence. For one thing, prayer is always in that circle.
An excellent way to deal with the myriad things in your sphere
of concern is to turn them into intercession. But there are other
things in your Circle of Influence to wield as well: how you
spend your time, what you do during family time, what you talk
about in the car, what you read to your kids at night, the kinds
of conversations you initiate, the one-on-one time you initiate
with your kids (and with Jesus). The pages ahead explore all
these topics.

One last thing: Were you able to locate the Circle of Control in
this visual? Oh, sorry—did you miss it? Turn the page and I'll highlight it for you:

There it is![5] This journey is one of recognizing and accepting the myriad things that are beyond our control—including, ultimately, the outcome of our children's spiritual journeys—and then intentionally choosing to direct our time and energy to our Circle of Influence rather than living from the realm of infinite concerns we cannot do anything about.

circle of concern

circle of influence

speck of control

The Serenity Prayer, faithful friend to many who have reckoned with the delicate balance between powerlessness and intentionality, comes to mind here:

> God, grant me the serenity to accept the things
>   I cannot change;
> the courage to change the things I can;
> and the wisdom to know the difference.
> Amen.

QUESTIONS FOR REFLECTION

1. How does it feel to think about preparing your kids to be misunderstood by the world around them? What thoughts or emotions does this bring up for you?

2. How does it feel to know that God trusts you and is inviting you to be part of his purposes?

3. What "ordinary moments" throughout your day already come to mind as moments that could be repurposed?

4. What encouragement can you draw from Daniel's story?

For pastors and church leaders

1. What would helping your church become a "creative minority" look like in your particular context?

2. How does your ministry intersect with God's larger purposes throughout human history? Do you have a sense that he is preparing you and your church for an outpouring of his Spirit?

3

THE GOOD NEWS

(Should You Choose to Accept It)

*For better or worse, parents are actually the
most influential pastors of their children. Parents
set a kind of glass ceiling of religious commitment,
above which their children rarely rise.*

CHRISTIAN SMITH

A T THE HEIGHT OF THE 1980S' WAR ON DRUGS, several television commercials aired during prime time designed to discourage teenage drug use. Perhaps you remember or have heard of the "This is your brain. This is your brain on drugs" fried-egg version. Most memorable to me, however, was the ad depicting a boy in trouble with his dad over a box of drug paraphernalia discovered in his closet. The dumbfounded dad begins to interrogate the boy and eventually asks, "Who taught you how to do this stuff?" The boy replies, "You, all right? I learned it by watching you!" The ad ends with the narrator explaining, "Parents who use drugs have children who use drugs."

This commercial has inspired numerous parodies, including a 2012 Kraft Mac and Cheese ad called "A Father's Lesson," which features a father scolding his son for "skimming" some orange noodles from his sister's plate, only to discover that he was the one who taught him how to do it: "Parents who skim mac and cheese have kids who skim mac and cheese." While the original commercial may have overplayed its hand with the ominous tone, the principle holds true: parents wield an incredible amount of influence when it comes to the behaviors and attitudes of their children.

This is our good news: there is one thing that makes a drastic difference in the 50 percent statistic. And it's not church attendance, Sunday school involvement, youth group participation, religious education, or the influence of church staff.

It's *you*.

Over the course of a decade, from 2003 to 2014, Christian Smith, professor of sociology at Notre Dame, led a massive research endeavor called the National Study of Youth and Religion. This study examined the relationship between childhood faith and adult faith. What Smith found was that parents were the number-one predictor of a child's spirituality throughout their lives.[1] This may seem surprising to you—especially if your kids don't enjoy being seen in public with you or could teach a Master-Class on the art of the eye roll. But it's true: you have more influence on their walk with Jesus than anyone else in their lives, including the "professionals." Your investment in their discipleship matters more than any program your church could offer. Now, this is not to diminish the importance of church programming and staff—you cannot expect to raise healthy disciples of Jesus without the church—but nothing compares to the influence of parents.

So this is really good news, friends. But channeling Billy Mays, the infomercial guy, "But, wait, there's more!" Because here's some even better news.

When it comes to whether kids will go on to follow Jesus as adults, Smith found that the single most significant parental behavior is actually incredibly simple. It doesn't take a seminary degree or years of practice to learn how to do it. It can be done anywhere, anytime. And, not surprisingly, it's very Deuteronomy 6. The parental behavior that makes the biggest difference in that 50 percent statistic is this: it's parents who talk about and practice their faith at home. As it turns out, 82 percent of children whose parents place great importance on their beliefs, are active in their churches, and talk about and practice their faith at home go on to follow Jesus as adults.

Eighty-two percent, friends. That is a far cry from the 50 percent statistic we've come to accept as normative, and this is very good news. Let's talk about why this might be.

PARENTS HAVE TIME

First of all, parents have time. Perhaps you just spit out your coffee from laughing so hard at this suggestion. Time—second perhaps only to sleep for those with very young children—may be the commodity you feel you have the least of these days. Between the juggling act of school routines, work schedules, after school activities, and a to-do list that never seems to end, it can feel like each day is a sprint from that early-morning wake-up to the moment you finally get to collapse that weary body of yours into bed.

And yet, when it comes to helping our kids learn to love and follow Jesus, comparatively speaking, parents have more time than anyone else. The average number of hours per year that a church has to influence a child is forty. If a child participates in Sunday school and youth group weekly, with perfect attendance every week of the year, maybe that number could jump as high as one hundred. But the average is forty.

Parents, on the other hand, have an average of three thousand hours per year with which to influence their kids. This number is averaged out from birth to eighteen. Obviously stay-at-home parents of infants have many more hours per year than parents of teenagers in school. But any way you slice it, even in split-custody situations, you still have exponentially more time to invest in your child's spiritual journey than your pastor, youth pastor, or their Sunday school teacher.

Whether you use this time for this purpose is up to you. Someone once told me that any time I was tempted to say, "I don't have time," I should try saying, "It's not a priority," instead and see how that felt. That one simple practice was transformative. I can't tell you how many times, while writing this book, I had blocked off precious hours in my schedule to write—often in the evenings after the kids were supposedly in bed—when one of them would venture out of bed and interrupt me with a spiritual question. It almost felt like a test. Replacing my inner monologue of "I don't have time for this" with "It's not a priority" changed how I felt about these interruptions, and I chose to prioritize them. Now, let me be clear: I am not talking about boundaries or bedtime or appropriate times to interrupt Mom. In your house, you may have rules around conversations that happen after bedtime, or when Mom is working, and it may be 100 percent appropriate to send that child right back to bed. The point I'm making is about becoming more aware when it comes to how we use our time, of what we prioritize and why.

Here's a tool that has helped me begin to recognize the often-unconscious priorities governing the use of my time. If you haven't noticed by now, I really like charts.[2] I find they have an elegance for visually depicting an idea in a way that brings new or clarified meaning. But if you find them limiting and restrictive, please skip the charts and hang on to the principles they demonstrate.

Visualizing priorities instructions. Using the chart in this section, compare the level of time, attention, and effort you devote to your child's development in the following areas. If you have multiple children, you might want to color code your answers.

Feel free to eyeball it with a simple ranking, or if you prefer a more scientific approach, use the following formula.

Time = Hours per week you spend on this area

Attention = Your level of thought and concern about this area (0 to 5)

Effort = Your level of personal involvement in this area (0 to 5)

For example, thinking about Noah, the Social row on our chart would have zeros for time, attention, and effort. We are past the age of playdates and matchmaking friendships for him, and he has enough neighborhood friends that we don't need to play chauffeur on account of his social life. But the Musical row would look very different. We often spend up to five hours per week of our time on Noah's musical pursuits: drum lessons, worship team practice, and getting him to church early when he's playing on a Sunday. Our level of attention is probably a three. We love that he is doing this, we are cheerleading him thoroughly, but we wouldn't be crushed if he decided to quit one day. Our level of personal involvement is probably a four. We have made some significant investments in drum equipment, and Greg often helps him learn new worship songs.

Feel free to consider other areas not listed here. (And for those who would rather not engage a chart, use the ideas here like a free-write prompt.)

Visualizing priorities reflection questions.

- What do you notice? Does anything surprise you?
- Is there anything you see here that you'd like to adjust?

Making discipleship a priority in your home won't happen without some intentional reordering of priorities on your part to devote a chunk of those three thousand hours (fifty-seven-ish per week) to spiritual rhythms and practices. For those of you just trying to make it to bedtime in one piece, this may sound overwhelming

VISUALIZING PRIORITIES

	TIME	ATTENTION	EFFORT	RANK
ACADEMIC helping with homework, tutoring, reading				
SOCIAL playdates, enrichment classes				
MUSICAL lessons, practice				
ATHLETIC practices, games				
ARTISTIC lessons, practice				
SPIRITUAL church activities, home discipleship				

and intimidating, especially in light of how many hours are already accounted for. But let me tell you some more good news: you don't need to magically locate more hours in the week to do this well. And it's possible you won't need to cut anything out either. Often, just like Deuteronomy 6 describes, one of the best strategies is to simply repurpose the time we already have.

So let me share another tool to help you begin to do this. On the following pages I've included an audit of your family time to help you think through your regular daily routines, mining for family time. We'll talk more about how to leverage these moments for discipleship in the following chapters. For now, just notice where these times naturally occur. (And again, for those who don't love charts as much as I do, consider the concepts here another free-write prompt.)

Family time audit instructions. Where do you notice family time and one-on-one time with each child already built into your week? Use each child's initials and "F" for family to identify these times.

FAMILY TIME AUDIT

	M	Tu	W
EARLY MORNING wake-up time, early risers			
MORNING breakfast, getting ready, morning routines			
MID-DAY lunchtime			
EARLY AFTERNOON naptime, playtime			
MID/LATE AFTERNOON after school, shuttling places			
EVENING dinner, bedtime routines			
LATE EVENING social time, older kids, babies			
MIDDLE OF THE NIGHT wake-ups, feedings			

These don't have to be intentional blocks of time, it's more likely they will be family or solo-kid times by default (think rides to school, dinnertime, and bath times). For example, in our home, the only weekday family time we have is during dinner and before bedtime. The rest of the blocks are blank. The kids typically wake up earlier than we do and get themselves out the door on their own. On weekends, however, we have lots of family time, and solo time with each of them while the other has drum lessons.

	Th	F	Sa	Su
Early AM				
AM				
Midday				
Early Aft				
Afternoon				
Late Aft				
Evening				
Late Eve				

Family time audit reflection questions.

- What do you notice? Does anything surprise you?
- Where do you see opportunities you were previously unaware of?

PARENTS HAVE SPIRITUAL AUTHORITY

In addition to time, the other thing parents have is spiritual authority. One simple definition of spiritual authority is the right to make use of God's power on earth. Think about how earthly authority works. A twelve-year-old bus monitor has the authority to write up her fellow students for misbehaving. She has the right to make use of the school's power in that situation. A crossing guard has the authority to stop traffic because he has the right to make use of the city's power in that situation. When it comes to spiritual authority, it's exactly the same: in certain situations, disciples of Jesus are given the right to make use of God's power on earth.

From Scripture, we know that all power and all authority belong to God (Romans 13:1; 1 Peter 5:11) and were given to Jesus (Matthew 28:18). Throughout the Gospels, Jesus invited his followers to share in his ministry and to do what he did. The disciples preached the gospel, healed the sick, cast out demons, and—most significant to this conversation—made disciples. When Jesus ascended into heaven, he instructed them to wait for the gift of the Spirit. At Pentecost, with the pouring out of God's Spirit, God entrusted the ministry Jesus began on earth to the church. Ordinary humans, empowered by the Spirit, now have the right to exercise God's power on earth (Matthew 28:19; Acts 1:8) when they are submitted to his will (Romans 8:7; James 4:7) and committed to his purposes.

You are one such disciple. I imagine you have no trouble believing that your pastor possesses spiritual authority to minister in the church, because he or she was called by God into that assignment. You might take it for granted that your pastor has the "right to make use of God's power" in their ministry of preaching, teaching, shepherding, and leading.

Well, guess what? You have been called by God to a specific ministry assignment as well! As followers of Jesus, we were given a calling the moment we became parents. Os Guinness says a calling is "our personal answer to God's address, our response to God's summons."[3] For parents, the summons in Scripture is clear. We are instructed to "Bring [our children] up in the training and instruction of the Lord" (Ephesians 6:4) and to "Direct [our] children onto the right path" (Proverbs 22:6 NLT). This assignment from God, to make disciples in the home, is no less legitimate than your pastor's assignment to make disciples in the church. Both are realizations of Jesus' instructions in Matthew 28:19-20 to "Make disciples of all nations, baptizing them in the name of the Father and of the Son and of the Holy Spirit, and teaching them to obey everything I have commanded you."

So as we submit ourselves to God and come under his authority in our lives—the same way the bus monitor submits to the school's authority—there's no reason that we shouldn't walk in spiritual authority as we pray for, teach, train, lead, and "direct our children onto the right path." As an agent of God's kingdom, on a specific assignment from God, you have the right to make use of God's power on earth. You can pray boldly for your children, the kind of prayers that make heaven and earth tremble. You can lead your children with courage and confidence because, just like the bus monitor or the crossing guard, you know who has given you this assignment and who will always have your back.

GROWING IN SPIRITUAL AUTHORITY

What if you feel like you have no idea how to find or use this authority you supposedly have access to? Is there a way to get better at walking in spiritual authority? Absolutely. We can learn a lot about how to grow in spiritual authority by looking at Jesus.

In the New Testament, the scribes and the Pharisees often wondered about where Jesus' authority came from. How was he able to heal the sick, cast out demons, and perform miracles? In John 5:19 Jesus tells them, "The Son can do nothing by himself; he can do only what he sees his Father doing." Why did Jesus have so much spiritual authority? Because he listened to the Father's voice and did whatever his Father told him. And, as Jesus told his disciples the night before he died, the same principle applies to us: "I am the vine; you are the branches. If you remain in me and I in you, you will bear much fruit; apart from me you can do nothing" (John 15:5). Just like the bus monitor, apart from her relationship with the school, would not be effective at her job, neither will we be effective at this task apart from our relationship with Jesus. It's our intimacy with God, our ability to hear and obey God's voice, that enables us to walk in spiritual authority.

In 2008, Greg and I took a group of college students to Uganda on an InterVarsity Global Project. The vision of this project was for the US team to come under the leadership of a local student movement called Focus Uganda. Rather than coming in with our own agenda, we wanted to learn from our Ugandan partners. So we committed to participate in whatever project the Ugandan students chose to do. Our idea for a "mission trip" would have been to paint a few houses or, if we were feeling ambitious, to build some houses. The Ugandan students had a different idea: they wanted to spend the week in an active war zone, doing "hut-to-hut" evangelism and healing ministry in a refugee camp from nine to five and then hosting evangelistic outreaches each evening.

The American students and staff were terrified, but in our mission-trip-done-right idealism we had committed to fully submit to local leadership. In other words, there was absolutely no getting out of it. Each day we piled onto a bus, paired our students up with a Ugandan partner, and sent them out two by two like the disciples in Luke 9. And we saw some absolutely remarkable things:

we saw physical healings, we saw demons manifest and come out of people, and we saw droves of people come to faith in Jesus.

And we couldn't help but ask ourselves why we'd never witnessed anything like this on our US college campuses. There were lots of ivory-tower-type theories about this, including the "spirituality" of the Ugandan culture or the desperation of life in a war zone. But then we began to notice something: At the end of each day, the American team went to bed, exhausted. But the Ugandan students stayed up all night, praying and seeking God. In the mornings, when we went hut to hut and demons manifested, the American team was terrified. But Ugandan students boldly cast those demons out. And in the evenings when hundreds of people pressed around us, the American team was overwhelmed. But the Ugandan students took the microphone and preached the gospel—and people came to faith.

These students had incredible spiritual authority, more than we'd ever seen before. And I believe one reason for this is that, like Jesus, they listened to the Father's voice and did whatever their Father told them to do. They sought God, they listened for his voice, and they obeyed.

Now you may not find yourself face-to-face with shrieking demons or open-air evangelism scenarios in your day-to-day parenting, but just imagine how walking in this kind of spiritual authority could influence your parenting: when your children have their own brushes with evil in the world, when their physical or mental health becomes compromised, when you find yourself needing to pray the kind of prayers that move mountains. If we want to walk in the kind of spiritual authority in our parenting that these students had in their day-to-day lives, it will require intimacy. We will need to learn to abide in Jesus, as he abides in us. We'll need to draw near to God, pursue him, and listen for his voice. If you don't know where to start, here's a simple practice to try. Start with five to ten minutes per day and gradually increase the time as you are able.

STEAL THIS IDEA: Ignatian Prayer

Also known as imaginative prayer, Ignatian prayer is a form of prayer that engages our imagination and helps us to encounter the Holy Spirit by reflecting on the person of Jesus.

Ages: Preschool and up

Supplies:

- Five to ten minutes alone in a quiet space (you may need help from a spouse, friend, or babysitter to locate this)
- Journal and pen
- Quiet music (optional)

Instructions:

- Settle into a comfortable position and close your eyes.
- Invite the Holy Spirit to meet with you today and to inspire your imagination to help you encounter God.
- In your mind's eye, picture somewhere you feel peaceful. Maybe it's a scene in nature, a favorite spot from your childhood, or somewhere imagined.
- Next, picture Jesus coming to join you in that place. Imagine him walking up to you. As he comes closer, simply watch what he does, listen for anything he says, and allow your imagination, led by the Spirit, to participate in the scene.
- Feel free to ask Jesus any questions that come to mind.
- Write down anything significant that Jesus says or does.
- When you are finished, read over what you've written down and test it against Scripture. If it contradicts anything you know about Jesus from Scripture, let it go. But if it fits with the nature and character of God, gently receive it. Consider sharing with some spiritually mature friends who can confirm that this sounds like God.

DOWN THE RABBIT HOLE

If we were ever tempted to outsource the spiritual development of our kids to the "professionals" before—for fear of not being capable enough, for lack of time, or for sheer lack of interest—we now know that's no longer an option.

The good news in this conversation comes with a clear invitation to offer back to God what God has already given you: your time, your influence, your love for your children, your creativity, and your willingness. I encourage you to offer these to Jesus the same way the little boy in John 6 offers his lunch to feed the multitudes. Without the power of God to multiply his five loaves and two fish, the crowds would have gone away hungry. In the same way, the things in your hands are not sufficient to satisfy your children's spiritual hunger and nourish their souls, but they are essential. If you've ever felt like you don't have enough—or simply *aren't* enough—for this journey, take heart. In Jesus' hands, a boy's humble lunch was enough to feed five thousand men, plus women and children. No matter how long you've been following Jesus or how rocky that journey has been, your humble efforts to talk about and practice your faith at home are more than enough in God's capable, powerful hands.

QUESTIONS FOR REFLECTION

1. How did this chapter make you feel? What invitations from God are you sensing right now?

2. What did you learn from the exercises regarding your priorities and your time? Can you boil it down to one or two takeaways?

3. What do you think about the idea that you have been given a specific ministry assignment from God? How does this idea intersect with your sense of calling and purpose?

4. How would you describe your relationship with Jesus in terms of its intimacy? Do you feel able to talk with God like you would with a friend? If not, what do you think is holding you back?

For pastors and church leaders

1. What are the implications of this "good news" for your church?

2. How does the organization and structure of your children's ministry support the idea that parents are actually "the most influential pastors of their children"?

4

RESPONSIVE DISCIPLESHIP

(or How to Catch a Kairos)

For you created my inmost being;
you knit me together in my mother's womb.

PSALM 139:13

We love because he first loved us.
1 JOHN 4:19

Earth's crammed with heaven,
And every common bush afire with God,
But only he who sees takes off his shoes;
The rest sit round and pluck blackberries.

ELIZABETH BARRETT BROWNING,
AURORA LEIGH

LONG BEFORE YOU LEARNED you were expecting a child or saw that first photo of your foster- or adopted-child-to-be, long before you held your grandchild in your arms, God was at work in your child's life. As we say yes to this discipleship journey, it's important to remember that God has known and loved our kids longer and more deeply than we ever will. I was never a "baby person" before I had my own. I remember walking around my neighborhood at forty-one weeks pregnant with our first son, crying my eyes out to my mom, worried I wouldn't know how to love a baby. My mom, though full of motherly empathy, couldn't suppress the amused sparkle in her eye as she said, "Oh honey, just you wait." And, as usual, Mom was right.

That overwhelming, gut-wrenching, irrepressible love I feel for my kids—that you undoubtedly feel for yours—is just a hint of an echo of a shadow of what God feels for them. And this is significant because it means that no matter how badly we want our children to know and follow Jesus, we can be certain that God wants it more. And no matter what we do to aid and assist them on this journey, we can rest in the fact that Jesus has already done, and will continue to do, more than we ever could.

In Matthew, Jesus uses the imagery of a yoke: "Take my yoke upon you and learn from me" (Matthew 11:29).[1] A yoke is the shoulder bar that binds two oxen together as they pull a plow. It keeps them in step with one another, helps them move at the same pace, and is also used to train young oxen by pairing them with an older, stronger, and more experienced ox. When it comes

to being yoked to Jesus, I love to remember that Jesus is always the older, stronger, more experienced ox. We may throw our weight into that yoke, pulling our hardest against the plow, and we may be encouraged by the progress we see as we move forward step by step. But in reality, Jesus is the one shouldering most of the load. His body bears the weight, his leadership guides our steps, his power moves us forward.

As you teach your kids to follow Jesus, I hope you will remember this image. You are the baby ox. Jesus is the one doing the work. Stay close to him, yoke yourself to him, and remember that he bears the weight.

One way we can remind ourselves of this reality is to learn to recognize and engage two different types of discipleship. One type of discipleship, the one probably most familiar to us, is what I would call proactive discipleship. These are the discipleship moments that we plan for and are intentional about—the habits, practices, and rhythms we invite our kids to engage with.

But before we do that, let's start by learning how to be responsive to discipleship moments we can't plan for—because they are moments that only God has planned for. The order here is important: starting with responsive discipleship before we move on to proactive discipleship is a small but meaningful nod to the fact that God is the primary initiator of spiritual growth.

KAIROS MOMENTS

Have you ever experienced a moment when you were sure that God was going out of his way to get your attention? God does this all the time with humans. From dreams to visions to signs and wonders to words spoken directly from his mouth to our hearts, God has been initiating with human beings since the beginning of human history.

These moments are sometimes referred to as "kairos moments," and here's why: There are two words for "time" in Greek. One is *chronos*, where we get the word chronology. This kind of time is linear, a straight line moving from the past to the present into the future. The other word for time is *kairos*. *Kairos* is used to describe a specific moment in time and a particular kind of moment; kairos moments are full of potential, ripe with opportunity and invitation. If we think about heaven and earth like overlapping spheres or dimensions, kairos moments happen when something of the heavenly realm breaks into the earthly realm.

When I talk to my kids about these moments, I call them "God moments"—moments when God interrupts life as usual, gets our attention, and invites us to respond to him in some way. (At one point we did refer to them as kairos moments, and Noah still talks about "catching a kairos.")

Sometimes God moments are dramatic and profound. A good example of that would be Moses with the burning bush. Moses, one of the great heroes of the Judeo-Christian story, was living a normal life as a shepherd. (Well, let's say relatively normal. Actually, he was hiding out after murdering someone. But, other than that, he was living a normal life.) And then one day, his status quo was dramatically interrupted. He was walking along with his sheep, minding his own business, when,

> There the angel of the LORD appeared to him in a flame of fire out of a bush; he looked, and the bush was blazing, yet it was not consumed. Then Moses said, "I must turn aside and look at this great sight, and see why the bush is not burned up." When the LORD saw that he had turned aside to see, God called to him out of the bush, "Moses, Moses!" And he said, "Here I am." Then he said, "Come no closer! Remove the sandals from your feet, for the place on which you are standing is holy ground." (Exodus 3:2-5 NRSV)

Moses' experience at the burning bush was a quintessential God moment. God interrupted Moses' life-as-usual; Moses "turned aside" to see what was happening and ended up having a profound encounter with God. This was the moment when God called Moses to return to Egypt to deliver God's people from slavery. This God moment shaped the trajectory of Moses' entire life—and, arguably, of human history—transforming him from a man hiding out in fear to the great deliverer of the Israelite people.

So sometimes God moments are epic and over the top. But often they come to us in more subtle and unassuming forms: a thought that strikes you out of a clear blue sky, an experience that impacts you in some unique way, a conversation that sticks with you long after it's over. With our kids, God moments can look like a surprising question they ask, a connection they make about God or the world, a dream they have, an intense emotion they can't quite explain (such as happy tears), an experience of guilt or forgiveness, an experience in worship—the list goes on.

One of the clearest examples of a God moment I can remember was when our younger son, Silas, who was four at the time, had received his fourth time-out in a row for questionable behavior during dinner. After apologizing and being forgiven for the fourth time, he returned to the table. His shoulders slumped over his plate, and he looked so sad. I asked him what was wrong, and he said, "My heart feels yucky." All of a sudden, I realized this was a God moment: I sensed God was trying to get our attention.

Whether these God moments will be powerful change-agents in our lives depends on our response to them. If we recognize the God moment (and we'll talk about how to do that in just a moment), we have two choices: we can either ignore the moment and continue on with life as usual, or we can "turn aside" like Moses and explore the moment with God. As we do this, we will discover discipleship opportunities hidden like buried treasure within these moments. In each God moment we will find specific ways that God is inviting us—and our kids—to be shaped and transformed by his Spirit.

Here's a visual to help us understand the process by which these God moments shape us:[2]

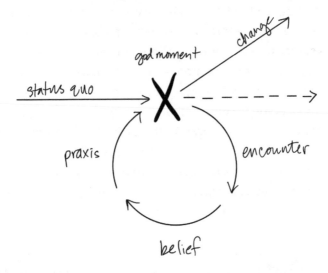

STEP ONE: IDENTIFY THE GOD MOMENT

The process begins with the horizontal arrow on the left. This is the status quo.

We are going about our normal daily activities, plodding along with one foot in front of the other, life as usual. This is Moses with his sheep or my family at dinnertime with very ordinary chicken nuggets and very ordinary four-year-old behavior.

Suddenly, a God moment interrupts us. Something of the kingdom of God breaks into the earthly realm in some way.

That may sound grandiose and complex, but it's really as simple as something getting our attention and causing us to become aware of God's presence in that moment. For Moses, this awareness of God was overpowering. He literally heard the voice of God coming from a bush that was on fire but not burning up. For me at the dinner table, it was much more subtle. I simply had the thought that Si's "yucky heart" sounded an awful lot like the conviction of the Holy Spirit. This fleeting thought turned my attention from chicken nuggets and time-outs to the Holy Spirit's activity in my son's life. And suddenly we found ourselves in the middle of a God moment.

Almost any moment, no matter how ordinary, can become a God moment if we simply pause and invite the Holy Spirit to meet us in the middle of it. Here are some examples of God moments our family has experienced in the midst of everyday life:

- Passing a homeless person on the street
- Hearing an ambulance or fire truck siren
- Wondering about what happens when you die
- A feeling of overwhelming peacefulness while kayaking
- Being hurt by a friend
- Being the recipient of a friend's incredible generosity
- Being anxious or afraid of something
- An experience of happy tears
- Realizing a friend doesn't know Jesus
- The death of a loved one

Each of these experiences served as a little burning bush for us—something in the earthly realm that got our attention and caused us to turn our hearts and our minds toward God.

Turn aside. Whenever we experience a God moment, we have a choice. We can let the moment pass by and return to life as usual—think

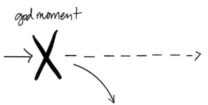

Peter returning to fishing in John 21—depicted by the horizontal arrow to the right of the God moment. Or we can choose to "turn aside" and explore the moment with God.

Rather than turning his attention back to his sheep, Moses chose to "turn aside and look at this great sight." Similarly, at my dinner table, I could have said, "Yeah, buddy, I'm not surprised your heart feels yucky," and directed our collective attention back to the half-eaten nuggets. Instead, recognizing a little burning bush in the form of Si's heavy conscience, I said, "Why don't you come sit in my lap and we'll talk to Jesus about it."

Sometimes you'll have time to "turn aside" for a nice rambling detour, and other times you may only have time for a quick pitstop. What matters is the intentional choice to respond, however you are able in the moment, to God's initiative when you recognize it.

I encourage you to use the "it's not a priority" test from chapter three here. When you identify a God moment but feel you can't turn aside, ask yourself, Is this actually true? Are you on mute during a video meeting, about to be called on to give your report to the board? Or is it merely inconvenient and unplanned, falling more in the "it's not a priority" camp? Could turning aside when you sense that God wants your child's attention be worth being five minutes late to school or telling the friend you're texting that you'll be right back?

My friend Corrie describes a time when, in the middle of dinner prep, she glanced over at her seven-year-old only to find her face stricken with fear. Harper, too scared and overwhelmed to talk about it, was replaying a frightening experience that had happened to her several weeks prior. What she did express was that she wanted to take some quiet time alone to read her Bible. Corrie watched her head upstairs, gave her a few minutes, then made a conscious choice to "turn aside," leaving the half-prepped dinner, to join Harper in her room. She affirmed Harper for her instinct to run to God when she was afraid and pointed her to Psalm 23. Corrie prayed for Harper and then let her continue to enjoy some alone time with Jesus.[3]

Training ourselves to identify God moments and to turn aside to explore them feels costly in the moment. Corrie knew dinner would be late that night. But learning to do this won't just benefit our kids—it will significantly deepen our own intimacy with God if we allow it to. How often do you and I miss God's presence with us throughout the day, even assuming God is absent, because we simply aren't looking for him? One of the beautiful realities about helping our kids to follow Jesus is that we will learn to follow Jesus in new ways as well. Being intentional to look for God's activity in the most ordinary of moments will remind us of God's constant, faithful, creative, persistent presence.

STEPS TWO THROUGH FOUR: EXPLORE THE GOD MOMENT

Once we turn aside, we have the opportunity to explore the moment with God. In the diagram you'll see a circular loop with three sections. Each section corresponds to a key ingredient of formation: Encounter, Belief, and Praxis.

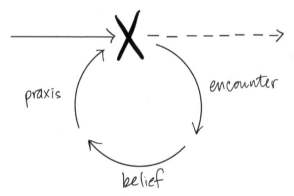

We can think of these ingredients as God's way of engaging our hearts (Encounter), our minds (Belief), and our feet (Praxis). The order of the steps is not important, and they don't have to happen all at once. Sometimes the experience of exploring a God moment can be stretched out over days or weeks. But each element is essential. Without Encounter, our faith has no warmth, and this can easily lead to the experience of "just going through the motions." Without biblical Belief, we can end up with some pretty warped—and dangerous—views about God and neighbor. Without Praxis, we have what happens in many churches on Sunday mornings: a powerful experience that doesn't make a bit of difference in terms of how we live the rest of the week.

Interestingly, each major stream of the church has one ingredient it especially gravitates toward. While each stream certainly has its flaws, each also offers a gift, or charism, to the wider church. We learn about intimate, powerful Encounter with God from our charismatic friends. Our evangelical[3] brothers and sisters contribute a passion for Scripture and doctrinal clarity (Belief). And our sacramental friends have much to teach us about Praxis—from classic spiritual disciplines to the rituals of church tradition, to faith in action in the form of pursuing justice.

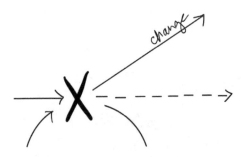

These three ingredients—Encounter, Belief, and Praxis—are what enable us to "catch" a God moment and, ultimately, to be changed by it. The goal of any type of discipleship is to allow the Holy Spirit to shape us—and our children—more and more into the likeness of Christ. This change is represented by the diagonal arrow traveling out of the circle on a different trajectory from the original arrow.

This is exactly what happens to Moses. Because of his experience with God at the burning bush, Moses the shepherd hiding in fear and shame becomes Moses the deliverer who courageously leads his people out of slavery in Egypt.

Let's continue to learn from Moses' experience by exploring each of the three ingredients in this loop—Encounter, Belief, and Praxis.

KEY INGREDIENTS OF A GOD MOMENT

	DEFINITION	MODE	CHURCH STREAM
ENCOUNTER	Direct interaction with God	Heart	Charismatic
BELIEF	Aligning our thinking with biblical truth	Mind	Evangelical
PRAXIS	Our partici-pation in our formation	Feet	Sacramental

ENCOUNTER

- Definition: direct interaction with God
- Mode of engagement: heart
- Church stream: charismatic

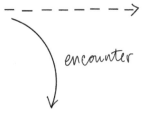

Moses had a powerful encounter with God at the burning bush. He did more than think about God or wonder about God while staring at the bush. He interacted with God directly, conversing with him, listening to him, and asking difficult questions. Humans were designed for intimate relationship with God. We see this intimacy depicted in Genesis—Adam and Eve walking and talking with God as they would a friend. The apostles enjoyed this kind of intimacy with Jesus, and by the Holy Spirit, this kind of intimacy is available to us as well.

And it's available to our kids—even to our infants. Yes, you read that right. It's true that little children are not yet abstract thinkers. But we sometimes assume that because they aren't capable of rationally comprehending God, they also aren't capable of interacting with God. If we follow this assumption to its natural conclusion, we expose some dangerous theological fallacies: Do we truly believe that possessing a sound, rational, thinking mind is the prerequisite for a meaningful relationship with God? What do we do with people with intellectual and cognitive disabilities, mental illnesses, or dementia? Our ability to know God has never been dependent on the capacity of our minds; to think otherwise is a harmful overinflation of our role in the relationship. For limited, finite human beings to interact with a holy, infinite God at all, humanity never bridges the gap; God draws near and makes himself known to us.

Given this reality—that God bridges an infinite gap to interact with human adults—it is not much of a leap to assume that God can interact with human children, even pre-verbal infants and toddlers, and that they can interact with him. The gap between human infant and human adult is minuscule compared to the gap between human adult and God—illustrated for you at the bottom of the page. What's more, Scripture tells us that "the Spirit himself intercedes for us through wordless groans" (Romans 8:26). While words and language can be helpful in a child's maturing expression of faith, human language is not the foundation of intimacy with God. It's simply the threshold at which parents begin to have a concrete window into their child's spirituality.

I recently spoke with the mother of an eighteen-month-old about this idea and a smile came over her face as we talked. "You know, it's funny," she said. "We read a lot of books with our

GOD
|
_____

daughter, and I've noticed that whenever we read this one board book about Easter, there's a certain page where she always gets really quiet. Her whole body calms down and she gets really still, just looking at the page for a long time before reaching out to turn it. She doesn't do that with any other books, just this one." Could this holy pause be an eighteen-month-old's way of responding to an encounter with the Holy Spirit through the story of Jesus? Absolutely! I am convinced there is no one that God cannot reach and communicate with, and that includes even our tiniest babies.

BELIEF

- Definition: right thinking about God, ourselves, and the world; and the correction of false beliefs
- Mode of engagement: mind
- Church stream: evangelical

belief

In addition to having a powerful encounter with God at the burning bush, Moses' thinking was refined and clarified. Before he could respond to God's invitation to return to Egypt, some of his critical beliefs needed to become aligned with God's truth—beliefs about himself and beliefs about God. Moses needed to hear from God that God could use him despite his past, his lack of confidence, and his difficulty speaking (Exodus 3:11; 4:1; 4:10). And Moses needed to know that God would be with him, what God's name was, and that God would have Moses' back by demonstrating his power through signs (Exodus 3:12; 3:14; 4:8).

Right thinking about God is just as important as our heartfelt intimacy with him. A. W. Tozer famously said, "What comes into our minds when we think about God is the most important thing about us."[4] As we explore God moments, we are invited to examine

human adult — *human baby*

what we believe—not just about God, but about ourselves, our kids, and the world around us—and allow Scripture to gently correct areas that are out of alignment. This is what Paul meant when he urged the church in Rome to "be transformed by the renewing of your mind" (Romans 12:2). The invitation is to allow Scripture to become our plumb line for what is true, good, and, ultimately, real. A plumb line was an ancient type of level, involving a lead weight tied to a string, used by builders to determine what true perpendicular was. Without a plumb line, "perpendicular" quickly becomes a matter of opinion based on one's particular perspective. In the same way, Scripture serves as our plumb line for what we think about everything that truly matters in life.

PRAXIS

- Definition: our participation in our formation
- Mode of engagement: feet
- Church stream: sacramental

praxis

As Moses continued to engage with God at the burning bush, his next move became glaringly obvious: he needed to return to Egypt. Had he not executed this crucial last step, he would have returned to sheep tending and there would have been no significant change in his life—or in the world around him. Moses' decision to act in obedience to God completes this transformative experience, sending him forward on a different trajectory.

Praxis invites us to put our money where our mouth is. Without Praxis, our discipleship remains in the realm of our inner world—our experiences with God, our thoughts about God—but fails to touch our everyday life. This is why James declares that "faith without deeds is dead" (James 2:26). How many times have I had a moving encounter with God during worship, or thought profound thoughts about God while listening to a sermon, but then failed to live differently in any way? In many Western churches,

Praxis is the missing ingredient for lasting spiritual growth and transformation. Just like learning to recognize God moments in kids' lives will teach us to recognize God at work in our own lives, helping our kids put into practice what they have learned and experienced about God will train us to do this as well.

The change in Moses' life—and the liberation of the entire nation of Israel—happened because God initiated with Moses at the burning bush. No one sat down with Moses to create a discipleship plan to prepare him to return to Egypt and go toe-to-toe with Pharaoh. God simply intervened in his life. Moses did, however, pay attention, deviate from his routine, and allow God to use this moment to change him.

In the next chapter we'll look at how to curate this kind of experience for our kids as we lead them through each step of this process. Because through yucky hearts and ambulance sirens and happy tears, I believe God is still lighting bushes on fire in our lives and in the lives of our kids.

QUESTIONS FOR REFLECTION

1. Whether related to parenting or not, what was the last God moment you remember experiencing in your life?

2. What happened and how did you respond?

3. Which of the three ingredients—Encounter, Belief, Praxis— can you identify in this experience?

4. What might keep you from noticing a God moment as it's happening? What might keep you from "turning aside" when you do recognize one?

5. Reflect on Encounter, Belief, and Praxis: Which one are you most naturally drawn toward? Which one tends to be the

weakest in your own walk with Jesus? How do you see these preferences playing out as you lead your kids?

6. Have you ever experienced a God moment with your child? What did you notice, feel, and learn from this experience?

For pastors and church leaders

1. How could this framework be helpful to you in your unique ministry context? Do you see uses or applications beyond discipling children?

2. Does your church tend to gravitate more toward Encounter, Belief, or Praxis? What are the implications of this?

5

YUCKY HEARTS AND ASLAN ANXIETY

Leading Our Kids Through God Moments

*You may have heard speakers
challenging you to "bring God to these children."
We seem to have failed to recognize that God
is already there and active. We need to open
our eyes and see where he is at work.*

KATHRYN COPSEY,
FROM THE GROUND UP

NOW THAT WE HAVE A GOOD GRASP on what a God moment is and how to "catch" one, let's talk about what it looks like to lead our kids through this experience. There are four simple steps to this process: (1) identify the God moment, (2) facilitate Encounter, (3) clarify Belief, and (4) encourage Praxis.

Since we've already discussed the process of identifying God moments in chapter four, this chapter will focus primarily on steps two through four. These steps aren't always linear, but I have found this order to be helpful when I'm leading my own kids through a God moment.

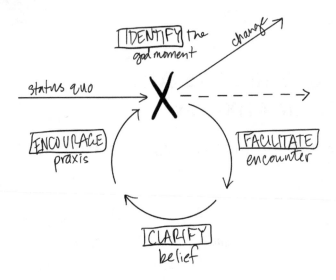

LEADING OUR KIDS THROUGH A GOD MOMENT

	DEFINITION	PARENT'S ROLE	KEY QUESTION
ENCOUNTER	direct interaction with God	facilitate	How can I help my child to interact directly with God?
BELIEF	aligning our thinking with biblical truth	clarify	How can I reinforce the learning with biblical truth?
PRAXIS	our partici-pation in our formation	encourage	How can I capture the learning with a practice or action step?

But first, let me say to parents of infants and toddlers, please don't tuck this chapter away until your kid is older. Now is the perfect time to train yourself to recognize and respond to God moments—both as they relate to parenting and to the other parts of your life. Remember, even the tiniest infant is capable of interacting with God. As you seek to encounter God yourself, you can absolutely invite God to speak to your baby right alongside you, even if you'll never get to hear about it.

STEP TWO: FACILITATE ENCOUNTER

- Definition: direct interaction with God

- Parent's role: facilitate

- Key question: How can I help my child to interact directly with God?

After we identify the God moment and turn aside, the next step is to facilitate Encounter. I use the word *facilitate* here with great intentionality. The goal of this step is to help our children interact directly with God—to speak to him and listen for his voice—without always going through us.

If we are honest, many of us would probably prefer to mediate these encounters rather than facilitate them. Mediating between our kids and God involves managing the relationship for them, while facilitating is a slight but intentional step to the side for the sake of fostering an independent relationship.

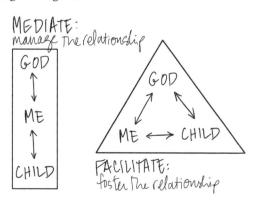

When I began writing this book, my mom was battling a horrific neurological disease called multiple system atrophy (MSA) that robbed her of both her mobility and her speech. The effects are similar to those of Lou Gehrig's disease. Google it if you're curious, and pray for a cure. Despite her loss of most physical function, Mom's mind remained strong and clear to the end. She even learned how, with great difficulty, to type short emails with her eyes using a retinal scanning device. In what would become our last email dialogue before she died, I asked her what one piece of advice she would give to parents learning to disciple their kids. This is what she said:

> I would say to parents who want to see their kids discipled: We are tempted to be a priest for our kids, telling God what the kid meant, and the kid what God meant. No. We should turn our children over to God as soon as possible. Get out of the way! That way, when the kid, as a natural part of growing up, rejects their parents' values, they won't reject God because God is theirs.[1]

Mom's point was that we are tempted to mediate, rather than to facilitate, our kids' relationship with God. There are several reasons for this.

Temptation One: Fear. We are afraid of unanswered prayer, difficult questions, doubts, and disappointment. We know these things are part of the spiritual journey—we have experienced them ourselves—and we want to protect our children from them as long as we can. We feel the need to provide clear explanations, and we worry about having all the "right answers." We assume that our carefully chosen words are the only thing standing between our children and the loss of their faith.

If you struggle with this kind of fear, I invite you to trust that God will meet you and your children in the midst of whatever challenges you may face on this journey. Consider the story of Jesus asleep in the boat while the disciples proceed to panic about the storm. They wake him up and ask, "Teacher, don't you care if we drown?" (Mark 4:38). Maybe the question rising in your throat is, "Jesus, don't you care if my kids lose their faith?" Maybe you feel exhausted from trying to explain the reality of unanswered prayer, suffering, or death to your children, much like the disciples were likely exhausted from bailing out their "nearly swamped" boat.

But then, Jesus "got up, rebuked the wind and said to the waves, 'Quiet! Be still!' Then the wind died down and it was completely calm" (Mark 4:39). In your context, the calming of the wind and waves might look like God speaking peace directly to your child's heart in a way that your words alone never could.

Temptation Two: Control. For some of us, learning to relinquish control is going to be a key struggle for our entire ~~discipleship~~ journey as parents. Mediating the relationship between God and our kids keeps us in the driver's seat, with our foot on the gas, navigating all the twists and turns. Often this looks like providing, or mandating, lots of spiritual activities—from church attendance to youth group involvement and church camps—without providing the tools the child needs for heart-level intimacy with God. This can lead to an overemphasis on external markers in the child's walk with God—good behavior, checking all the right boxes, doing all the right things—at the expense of true Encounter.

If this is your struggle, I invite you to rest in the knowledge that God is God, and you are not. Control is often just fear that knows how to lead. Underneath that put-together hustle is an anxious heart that doesn't know how to rest. Instead, allow Jesus to lead you as you lead your kids. Remember that you are the baby ox in this relationship—Jesus is the only one truly in control—and receive these familiar words from him: "Come to me, all you who are weary and burdened, and I will give you rest. Take my yoke upon you and learn from me, for I am gentle and humble in heart, and you will find rest for your souls. For my yoke is easy and my burden is light" (Matthew 11:28-30).

Temptation Three: Disbelief. Finally, many of us don't believe that our children can interact with God directly in the ways I'm describing. We can't imagine that a three-, four-, or even twelve-year-old could learn to hear and recognize God's voice. Deep down we assume the things kids claim to experience in this area are either products of their own imaginations or simply fascinating coincidences. But when we examine these assumptions more closely, following them to their natural conclusion, we discover a parallel assumption that God is incapable of interacting with our children.

If you struggle to accept the idea that God could speak directly to your child, my invitation to you is twofold. First, take some time to explore why you struggle to believe this. Where did this idea come from? You may want to reflect on the story of young Samuel in 1 Samuel 3. In this story, Eli gives us a beautiful picture of what it looks like to facilitate a relationship between God and a child. Samuel hears God's voice in the night but is too young to recognize the voice as God's and assumes it is Eli's. When Eli eventually realizes what's going on, he doesn't insert himself into Samuel's experience. He simply tells Samuel who is actually calling him and how he should respond: "Speak, LORD, for your servant is listening" (1 Samuel 3:9). Samuel does this, and God speaks very clearly and directly to him.

The second invitation is to take a page from Eli's book and simply see what happens when you set the stage for your children to interact directly with God. What do they report? What do you notice? What do you learn? Could it be worth a try? My friend Lisa's nine-year-old son had a bit of a meltdown one day as he struggled to catch a football during a family game. He became frustrated and overwhelmed, storming off in a fit. Instead of giving him a pep talk, Lisa encouraged him to take a few minutes to cool off and to talk to God about how he was feeling. When she checked on him a bit later, his entire demeanor was different. His eyes lit up as he said, "Mom, God spoke to me! As I looked out the window and watched you guys drop the football like five times in a row, I heard God's voice say, 'Everybody fails.'" With that, he collapsed into Lisa's arms in tears, in what she describes as a moment full of vulnerability and of the Spirit's power at work in his life.[2]

Now, to be clear, there is an important way that God invites us to participate as he connects with our kids. Helping our kids to understand God and his world is part of the ministry he has entrusted to us. But where mediation might look like standing in between our child and God and acting like a translator, facilitation looks like standing side by side, holding our kid's hand, experiencing God together, and gradually fading into the background as they begin to foster an independent relationship with God.

So how do we do this? How do we facilitate Encounter?

Let's return to my dinner table and the "yucky heart." Silas willingly agreed to come sit in my lap and talk to Jesus about what was going on. With shoulders still drooped, he walked around the table, climbed up in my lap, and melted into my chest. I asked him to close his eyes and invited the Holy Spirit to talk to him. I encouraged Silas to try to picture Jesus in his mind and to notice anything Jesus said or did. We sat in silence for a short while and then I asked, "Can you see Jesus, buddy?" He said he could. "What's he doing?" Greg and I waited with bated breath, hoping the answer wasn't something like "farting on my head."

Instead, Silas said this: "He's taking my yucky heart away and giving me a new one."

Tears sprang to my eyes. I was overwhelmed with thankfulness to Jesus for speaking so clearly to my little buddy! Mediating this encounter would have looked like me praying *for* Silas. In Lisa's case, it would have looked like giving her son a pep talk about his football skills, sprinkled with some encouraging Bible verses. And there's nothing wrong with praying for and over our kids or sharing Scripture with them. We should do that, and frequently! But in the yucky heart scenario, if I'm completely honest, my prayer probably would have focused on helping Silas to behave. I never would have thought, in that moment, to invite Jesus to take Si's yucky heart and give him a brand-new one. Only Jesus was able to do that for him. Learning to facilitate these encounters will help our children to experience more of Jesus than we'll ever be able to expose them to on our own.

Here's another example. When my oldest son Noah was seven, we introduced him to the Narnia series. He devoured *The Lion, the Witch, and the Wardrobe* in less than a week. The night he finished it, our friends Sarah and Shin were visiting. Sometime after bedtime, Noah came out into the living room and announced that he'd finished the book. We were so excited to help him make the connection between Aslan and Jesus and to see the extended metaphor in the story.

Noah was initially fascinated, but his fascination soon turned to dread. He started to panic. "Wait, if C. S. Lewis wrote this story about Aslan and it's not real, how do I know the story of Jesus is real? What if the authors of the Bible just made up those stories too?!" He was distraught. We tried to comfort him, but within a few short minutes he exclaimed, "I don't think I believe in God anymore."

This is a terrifying thing to hear from the lips of your child. Honestly, if Sarah and Shin weren't with us, I'm not sure we would have kept our cool the way we did. Partly because we had an audience, and partly by God's grace, we did not externalize our anxiety but decided to lead Noah through the same process we led Silas through at the dinner table.

We asked Noah to come sit with us and talk to Jesus about how he was feeling. We asked him to close his eyes, to picture Jesus in his mind, and to have a conversation with him. We encouraged him to tell Jesus what was bothering him. So he told Jesus, "I don't know if you're real anymore." We sat in silence for a while, the four adults praying silently and fervently, and Noah listening patiently. Eventually Noah opened his eyes and said, "Jesus said, 'Are you with me, Noah?'" To be honest, this wasn't what any of us expected to hear. We encouraged Noah that it was wonderful that he heard God's voice, and in a flash of pure brilliance Greg said, "You know what, buddy. It's late. Let's talk more about this in the morning when our minds are more awake." This afforded us some much-needed space to pray and process without the pressure of Noah waiting for us to make sense of it all.

In this scenario, mediating the relationship would have looked like calming Noah's fears with our own words, giving him "proof" of biblical authorship, reminding him of everything he had experienced of God's presence up to that point. And we did some of that. I'm not saying that kind of leadership isn't important. But in this situation, the key in Noah's breakthrough (which I'll describe shortly) was a simple word spoken directly from God's mouth to his heart. We facilitated Encounter by helping Noah listen for God's voice in the midst of his doubt and confusion. He could not have interpreted what he heard from God without our help, but we would not have been able to lead him through his swirling sea of doubts without God's intervention in the form of that word.

The following imaginative prayer practice is what we used in both these examples to facilitate Encounter between our kids and Jesus. I think this is a wonderful way to invite our kids to begin forming an independent relationship with God, and we have used this practice since they were around age three. But this is only one way of helping your kids to encounter God. Many times, facilitating Encounter simply involves inviting our kids to vocalize their thoughts directly to God instead of to us, giving them space to connect with God through Scripture like Corrie did for Harper in chapter four, or encouraging some other creative way of interacting with God.

For example, my friend Hope finds that her six-year-old daughter is hesitant to pray out loud but is a prolific prayer journaler. While her verbal prayers are typically limited to "thank you God for ..." or "we pray for so-and-so," her written prayers in response to simple prompts include beautiful expressions of worship, confession, and intercession.[3] The specific method we use is not nearly as important as the intentionality to create space for our kids to interact directly with God in their own unique ways.

STEAL THIS IDEA: IMAGINATIVE PRAYER

You can pull this practice out in the middle of a God moment, like we did with our boys, or it can become a regular practice that you work into your planned discipleship rhythms. For a wonderful resource that utilizes this practice, check out Jared Patrick Boyd's book, *Imaginative Prayer.*[4]

Ages: preschoolers and up

Supplies:

- A couple moments of quiet
- A cozy spot, with a blanket and pillow (optional)
- Calming music (optional)

Instructions:

- Invite your child to find a quiet, cozy spot.
- Put on some soft instrumental music. If this is a regular practice, you could consider using the same music every time to trigger a wind-down response.
- Explain the practice. Tell your child, "We are going to use our imagination to talk to Jesus!"
- Lead your child through the practice (three to five minutes max).
  - Invite them to close their eyes.
  - Invite them to picture Jesus in their mind. Maybe they are taking a walk together or sitting in a favorite spot together.
  - Invite them to ask or tell Jesus anything they'd like to.
  - Ask them to notice anything that Jesus says or does in response.
  - Invite them to open their eyes.
- Invite your child to share anything they saw or heard.
- Test it against Scripture and what you know to be true of God. If what Jesus says or does reminds you of a Bible verse or story, share that! As long as it sounds like Jesus' character and doesn't contradict anything you know

from Scripture, close the time by thanking Jesus for speaking to your child.

What to do if your child experiences Jesus doing something that doesn't sound like Jesus or contradicts Scripture:

- If it's simply something silly and innocuous, don't worry about it. One time, Silas told us that Jesus turned into a giant talking tooth. We just laughed and said, "Oh, that Jesus is pretty silly, isn't he!"

- If they report something that sounds wrong—such as Jesus shaming the child or saying something categorically untrue—it's best to be direct. You could say something like this: "Well, I'm not sure that was Jesus saying that to you, honey. I know Jesus wouldn't say you're a stupidhead because the Bible tells us that God is love, and that doesn't sound very loving, does it. Do you want to try listening again?"

Learning to facilitate Encounter as early as you can will serve you, and your kids, so well as they grow. As my mom reminded us, kids asserting their independence from parents is a natural part of growing up. But by helping them to develop their own relationship with Jesus as soon as possible, "they won't reject God, because God is theirs."

STEP THREE: CLARIFY BELIEF

- Definition: aligning our thinking with biblical truth

- Parent's role: clarify

- Key question: How can I reinforce this learning with biblical truth?

The next step is to clarify Belief for our kids—to help them evaluate what they believe about God, themselves, and the world against the plumb line of the Bible. Sometimes this involves pointing them to a specific verse or story from Scripture. Other times, clarifying Belief simply involves reminding our kids of God's character or fundamental truths about the world that we know from Scripture. For example, when a God moment stems from a child's Christlike response to something—mercy, compassion, generosity—clarifying Belief often looks like the simple affirmation that their response is not only honorable and good but also Christlike.

Returning to our dinnertime God moment, Silas had just told us that Jesus was taking his yucky heart and giving him a new one. From across the table Greg chimed in: "Silas, that sounds exactly like something Jesus would do. Did you know, in the Bible, God says that he will take away people's yucky hearts and give them new ones? Ezekiel 36:26 says, 'I will give you a new heart and put a new spirit in you; I will remove from you your heart of stone and give you a heart of flesh.'" Greg was able to affirm that what Silas experienced in prayer was 100 percent consistent with what we knew to be true about God from Scripture.

Now, whenever I tell this story, I am quick to point out that Greg has a near-photographic memory and the best Scripture recall of anyone I know. I would not have been able to pull up the chapter and verse like that, though I did recognize the image. The more time we spend with Scripture ourselves, the more we will remember the ideas and concepts we can use to reinforce, or correct, our children's developing beliefs (and we can always ask Siri or Alexa—or, in my case, Greg—for help with the reference).

Let me pause right here and bring you back to our Grace/Challenge Matrix, illustrated again for you below. Take note of which quadrant you're operating out of right now. If you need to take a moment to readjust and relocate yourself in the Freedom quadrant, I encourage you to do that before continuing.

While no one needs a theological degree to lead our kids through God moments, I do think that being intentional about

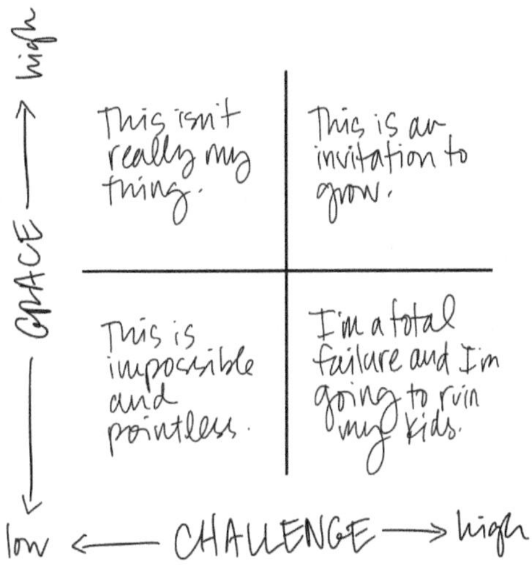
high
GRACE
low
This isn't really my thing.
This is an invitation to grow.
This is impossible and pointless.
I'm a total failure and I'm going to ruin my kids.
CHALLENGE
high

the Belief step will naturally raise the bar on our own level of biblical literacy. Whenever I hear something like "I feel like I barely know the Bible. How am I ever going to know what to say in these God moments?" come from the mouth of a parent, I always say three things:

1. Just start reading the Bible! Don't sign up for a seminary class, spend hundreds of dollars on commentaries, or throw your hands up and quit because you feel insecure or under-resourced. Just invest in your own discipleship by starting with a basic Bible reading plan. Take the first step.
2. Realize you don't need to have something amazing to say in the moment. "That's a good question—I'm really not sure" is always an acceptable answer. While we might feel under the gun in the moment, there isn't really any urgent time pressure. Coming back to our kids in a day or two, or even in a week, to restart the conversation is completely fine.

3. Remember that you have an unlimited number of "phone a friend" lifelines. When you are completely stumped, know that you can always text your pastor or a trusted friend for help. None of us can do this alone.

This is exactly what we did when Noah, listening for God's voice in his moment of doubt, heard something we couldn't immediately make sense of: "Noah, are you with me?" Encouraging him to head to bed with the assurance that we'd talk more in the morning afforded us the luxury of extra time to pray, process with friends (who happened to be in the room with us), and wrack our brains.

As we talked, I suddenly thought about John 15:4: "Abide in me as I abide in you. Just as the branch cannot bear fruit by itself unless it abides in the vine, neither can you unless you abide in me" (NRSV). Could the question that Noah heard from God, "Noah, are you with me?" be a seven-year-old version of, "Noah, abide with me"? We slept on it, and in the morning, this is what I told Noah: "You know how every season we clean out your dresser and give away the clothes that don't fit you anymore? If we never did that and you tried to wear the same clothes that you used to wear when you were three, it would probably be really uncomfortable and funny looking. I'm wondering if the same thing might be happening with the ways you interact with God. The things that helped you connect with God when you were three might be getting a little 'small' for you. I think when God asked, 'Noah, are you with me?' he might be asking for more time with you, and a deeper connection, so that you can feel closer to each other. I have an idea for how you could do that, but it's a surprise. I'll show you after school."

Like our experience with Silas at the dinner table, by testing Noah's word from God against Scripture, we were able to affirm that what he heard was indeed God's voice. We interpreted the word for him and helped him know what to do with it. In this case, it took a little more time and required a pause in the conversation to do this well—and that was completely fine and didn't inhibit the learning at all.

As we clarify Belief for our kids, we are modeling how to use Scripture as a plumb line. We are demonstrating that everything we think about God, ourselves, and the world is shaped and influenced by an external source of truth. And we are helping them to learn to love God not just with their hearts but also with their minds.

STEP FOUR: ENCOURAGE PRAXIS

- Definition: our participation in our formation
- Parent's role: encourage
- Key question: How can I capture the learning with an intentional practice or action step?

Praxis is what takes a God moment from being a powerful one-off experience and allows it to continue to affect us in an ongoing way. It can be as simple as asking the question, "What should we do about what God is saying?" or "What is one next step we could take?" Sometimes Praxis looks like a one-time action step, and other times Praxis looks like a new practice that makes its way into your life in an ongoing way.

For Silas, after his experience of receiving a new heart from Jesus, we decided to weave this idea into our time-out "liturgy." After receiving a time-out and discussing the infraction, we always end with an "I'm sorry" from the child and an "I love you and I forgive you" from the parent or sibling. (We use the same liturgy when parents need forgiveness too, by the way.) So, for a season, after forgiveness was extended, we would invite Silas to give his yucky heart to Jesus and ask for a new one. What this did was help him move from merely making amends with us, to learning to confess his sin directly to God and receive God's grace and forgiveness as well.

To summarize, here's how we led Silas through this God moment:

1. Identify the God Moment: When Silas said he had a "yucky heart," we recognized that God was initiating with him and paused to explore the moment.

2. Facilitate Encounter: We didn't just pray for Silas or talk to him about his yucky heart, we also created space for Silas and God to interact directly through imaginative prayer.

3. Clarify Belief: We tested Silas's experience of God against the truth of Scripture and affirmed that they aligned. We reinforced his subjective experience with objective truth.

4. Encourage Praxis: We built this practice into our apology "liturgy" to encourage confession to God.

For Noah, after our breakfast conversation, I sent him off to school in good spirits with the promise of a surprise when he returned home. While he was gone, I went to the store. I bought him a special candle, a journal, a new Bible, and *Jesus Calling: 365 Devotions for Kids* by Sarah Young (which I highly recommend). I dusted off an old coffee table from the basement and set it up in our office near a window. I hung some artwork in the window and put some examples of God's creation (a plant, some Rhode Island seashells) on the table, along with the candle, journal, Bible, devotional, and a holding cross (a small wooden cross carved in such a way that it fits perfectly in the palm of your hand). I also spread out some art supplies.

When he got home, I introduced him to his new "special God time" table. (I dislike calling devotional times "quiet times" because I believe it communicates the wrong message to kids who have not yet acquired a taste for silence and solitude.) I explained to Noah that these were "bigger kid" ways of connecting with God. I told him I would trust him to light a candle (and not burn the house down) to make it feel special. I showed him the artwork to reflect on, the plants and shells to touch and remember God's creativity, and the art supplies to reflect God's creativity. I showed him how to use the holding cross as a physical reminder to hold onto Jesus. And I encouraged him to use the new journal to keep an ongoing record of his conversation with God.

I told him that I would commit to spending twenty minutes with him after school for parallel special God time. We could put some "Jesus music" on and spend time with God together. He was thrilled and we started our practice that day. He drew a picture of Jesus calming the storm, wrote some prayers in the journal, and listened for God to speak back. We continued this practice daily.

A couple weeks later, I was so curious to know whether there were any updates on Noah's larger questions about God's existence. I had been afraid to push so hadn't brought it up yet, but I could no longer contain my curiosity. So as coolly and nonchalantly as an anxious mom can pretend to be, I asked, "Hey buddy, how are you doing with your bigger God questions?"

He answered back, just as nonchalantly, "Oh you mean whether or not God is real? I know he's real. He talks to me every day."

Our joint special God time practice didn't last forever, but it was just what Noah needed to learn how to abide with Jesus. Again, to summarize, here is how we led Noah through his God moment:

1. Identify the God Moment: We recognized God's initiative within the terrifying statement, "I don't know if I believe in God anymore."

2. Facilitate Encounter: We trusted God to speak to Noah for himself, rather than simply trying to convince Noah of God's existence.

3. Clarify Belief: We interpreted the word that Noah heard and helped him to understand what God was asking of him.

4. Encourage Praxis: We set up a space for Noah to abide with Jesus, in response to the invitation he heard from God.

STEAL THIS IDEA: SPECIAL GOD TIME SPOT

Ages: elementary school (readers and writers)

Supplies:

- Cozy nook somewhere private
- Ways to engage the mind—journal, devotional, Bible
- Ways to engage the senses—artwork, art supplies, candles or Christmas tree lights, worship music, holding cross, items from nature (plants, shells, etc.)

Instructions:

- Set up a special spot somewhere in the house that can remain set up—a little table in their room, a "tent" or other cozy nook, etc. You could either set it up by yourself and surprise them or involve the child in designing the space.
- Explain the idea of "special God time": time spent connecting with Jesus, sharing our thoughts with him, getting to know him better, receiving his love.
- Explain the different items and how to use them to connect with God:
  - A Bible to read about God
  - A journal to share your thoughts and feelings with God, and also to write down anything he says back
  - Art and items from nature to look at and think about God
  - A holding cross to touch and remind yourself to keep holding onto God
  - Art supplies to express your feelings about God creatively
  - Music to help you to connect with God in worship
- Invite (or challenge) your child to spend ten to twenty minutes a day connecting with Jesus. Offer to have your own special God time alongside them or to help them get started.

STEAL THIS IDEA: PRAYER JOURNALING

Consider doing this practice alongside your child. It could be something you do together for a while until they are able to do it on their own. Or it could become a family practice where everyone journals together (see chapter eleven).

Ages: elementary and older (readers and writers)

Supplies:

- Journal and pen
- Art supplies (optional)
- Music (optional)

Instructions:

- Put on some worship music (optional).
- Find a quiet spot and limit distractions.
- Set a timer. Start small (five to ten minutes) to aim for wins.
- Explain the practice to your child. You could say something like this:

This journal is just for you and God. No one else will read it unless you invite them to. Think of it as your way to say anything you want to God. Tell him what you're thinking about. Ask him questions. Talk to him like you would talk to a friend.

Then, listen. I believe God speaks to us, not usually in an audible voice, but often in our minds and thoughts. If you think God is saying something back to you as you write, write down what you hear. If you're unsure whether it's actually God speaking to you, feel free to show it to me and we can talk about it.

- Open and close the time with prayer.
- When you are finished, share about your experience and ask about theirs (but do not require that they share).

My kids aren't the only ones this four-step process has been helpful for. Let me return to Corrie and Harper, the story I began in chapter four, to demonstrate how Corrie used this model to shepherd Harper through a God moment.

1. Identify the God Moment: Corrie recognized God's tender initiative with Harper immediately. Given the emotional delicacy of this moment, she quickly rallied some prayer support by texting two of Harper's "spiritual moms" to ask them to pray. In her own words, "Texting them helped me feel like I wasn't navigating this precarious emotional state by myself. It reinforced that even if I don't get it perfectly in this moment, other people are on the same page and can scoop her up at some point and help interpret for her. It made me feel covered, like the pressure isn't all on me and on this particular moment."[5]

2. Facilitate Encounter: When Corrie checked on Harper a few minutes later, she pointed her to some helpful Scriptures to read and prayed for her, but she ultimately allowed Harper the space to spend time with Jesus on her own. "The shift that was important for me in that moment was recognizing her ownership. I realized maybe she wasn't ready to talk to me about the incident yet, but that she could absolutely talk to God about it."[6]

3. Clarify Belief: Later on, Harper came down from her room, relaxed and ready to talk. She was able to express to Corrie the specific lingering fears from the incident. Corrie helped her to identify where Jesus was when this happened and reminded her of God's constant presence and protection. They also talked about how helpful it was for Harper to run straight to God when she didn't know what to do or say.

4. Encourage Praxis: Through this experience, Corrie has set Harper up with a helpful, spiritually rich way to cope with

overwhelming feelings. The next time Harper is too over-whelmed to process, she'll know she can grab her Bible, find a quiet spot, and run straight to Jesus.

IT WORKS IF YOU WORK IT

To borrow a phrase from the recovery community, "It works if you work it." I absolutely love this four-step method of responding to God moments and use it regularly with my kids. But even though I've walked them through the process countless times, I still need to be intentional about each step. I need to make a conscious choice to put down what I'm doing and "turn aside." I need to work at not putting myself in the middle of their conversations with God. I need to think about what truth to reinforce, what Scripture story to tell, what to say in the moment. And I especially need to be intentional about following through with a concrete practice. It takes work. But, truly, it works if you work it. Just like dancers using step charts stenciled on the floor eventually don't need to look down to dance, I promise you won't need to keep pulling out the diagram once you've walked through the process a few times. You'll learn the rhythm and internalize the steps. And, over time, you'll begin to see yourself and your kids emerging on the other side of these God moments looking more like Jesus, knowing and loving him a little bit more, and understanding more of his kingdom and purposes in the world.

This week, see if you can identify a God moment and make it all the way around the circle. This could be with a child, or even just by yourself. I'm confident there are burning bushes hiding in plain sight all over your world—in your kitchen, in the playground, in your car, under your kid's bed, or in a text thread. Because Moses the shepherd chose to turn aside and explore one particular moment with God, Moses the deliverer freed an entire nation from slavery and changed the course of human history. Who could you and your children be tomorrow—and what could God do through you in the world because of a God moment you notice today?

QUESTIONS FOR REFLECTION

1. Which step feels the most natural to you? The most challenging?

2. Facilitate Encounter: In what ways, or in what situations, are you tempted to mediate Encounter for your kids? Do you resonate with any of the common reasons we do this—fear, control, or disbelief? What is God saying to you about this?

3. Clarify Belief: How comfortable do you feel doing this with and for your kids? What is one way you could grow in this area?

4. Encourage Praxis: In your own life, what helps you to take what you experience of God in your own heart and mind and walk it out with your feet? What will it take to help your kids do this?

5. If you do lead your kids through a God moment this week, reflect on it. What happened? What did you learn? What was the fruit? Was there anywhere you got stuck? What would you do differently next time? Thank God for what you and your kids are learning.

For pastors and church leaders

1. In your particular context, do you see any potential applications for this four-step process beyond the discipleship of children?

2. In your leadership role, which step comes the most naturally to you? Which steps feels the most awkward or weakest for you as you lead?

6

PROACTIVE DISCIPLESHIP

(or Grilled Cheese and the Way of Jesus)

*Remember that you are not called to produce
successful, upwardly mobile, highly educated,
athletically talented machines. . . . Giving
your children great opportunities is good;
it is not, however, the goal of parenting.
Christlikeness is. Above all, seek to raise
children who look and act a lot like Jesus.*

**CHIP INGRAM, *EFFECTIVE PARENTING
IN A DEFECTIVE WORLD***

*I have no greater joy than to hear that
my children are walking in the truth.*

3 JOHN 4

After my mom was diagnosed with MSA but before she lost her ability to communicate, she sat down and wrote a letter to my sister, Betsy, and me. Instead of giving it to us, she tucked it away in a white binder labeled "Spiritual Legacy." Inside were instructions for her funeral, some personal reflections on the end of life, and this letter. One evening when I was visiting, she showed me the binder and asked me to pull it out after she died. I didn't think about it again until the day we returned from the hospital without her. As we began to discuss funeral plans, I remembered that white binder. But when I mentioned it to my dad, he had no idea what it was or where it might be. Feeling a little panicky, I went to the spot in the dining room where she had placed it three years earlier—and, unbelievably, it was still right where she left it.

It was an exquisitely beautiful letter, full of love and hope, humor and courage. I am convinced that every ill or aging parent should plan to give their children the gift of their own voice to shepherd the child through that initial shockwave of grief.

I'd like to share one paragraph of Mom's letter with you:

> I hope you know that as proud as I am of your academic achievements, your careers, your relationships, your children, and your good works, the thing that amazes and delights me more and more is your love for and obedience to our Lord and Savior Jesus Christ. It will always be difficult to keep the faith; at times more than ever—life has a way of getting in the way. But the Lord who died for you, and whom God raised from the dead, has power to keep you by His side. I guess my one word of advice is this: Abide in Him. You know my "life verse" is this: 3 John 4: "I have no greater joy than this, to hear my children are walking in the truth." As with John, the author, this applies to my nonbiological, but spiritual "children" of course, but your faith is of particular joy to me! If that puts any pressure on you, I apologize. I don't mean to obligate you but to give you freedom to enjoy the best relationship in my life.[1]

What I see so clearly in this paragraph are Mom's priorities as a mother. Of all the things she taught Betsy and me, and of all the things we've "accomplished" in life, she was proudest of our faith in Jesus. And this wasn't just true as she sat and reflected on "how we turned out." This was true every single day of her journey as a mother. Her words here have so much integrity because they perfectly reflect the intentionality of her spiritual leadership in our lives throughout our childhood and into our adulthood. My friend Jason Gaboury, who has also parented with this type of intentionality, says, "Sometimes I joke that some families do soccer, some families do music, and we do life with God. That's just what we do."[2]

According to a recent Pew Research Study, 89 percent of Christian[3] parents of teenagers in the United States feel it is very important that their children work hard, and 72 percent feel it is very important that their children go to college. But only 56 percent of these same parents feel it is very important that their children are raised to follow Jesus.[4] I can't help but think about the 50 percent "bad news" statistic from chapter one when I read these statistics. If every Christian parent had my mom's laser-focused clarity on what really matters in life, would we still find ourselves in this position?

This is where proactive discipleship comes in. If responsive discipleship is responding to God's initiative with our kids, proactive discipleship is an invitation from God to engage the process of discipleship through our own thoughtful and creative initiative.

PATHWAYS OF DISCIPLINED GRACE

The hallmark of proactive discipleship is cultivating an intentional way of life that revolves around consistent, deliberate spiritual practices. Let me first address some common misconceptions about spiritual practices.

In chapter four, I described how each major stream of the church—charismatic, evangelical, and sacramental—tends to gravitate toward a different ingredient of formation. Charismatic churches have the most to teach us about Encounter, evangelical churches often gravitate toward a more intellectual expression of biblical Belief, and sacramental churches often have the most concrete Praxis. Sometimes, based on what our particular church tradition tends to emphasize, we can end up with an under-developed experience of one or more of these ingredients. This can lead to very different ways of entering the conversation about spiritual practices.

For example, some friends of mine raised in the sacramental stream of the church with an underdeveloped experience of En-counter feel immediately allergic to the concept of spiritual prac-tices because their experience of them lacked the warmth of true intimacy with Jesus. Perhaps you remember mechanically re-citing a certain number of Our Fathers and Hail Marys after con-fession or making your way through the "Catholic calisthenics" of Sunday Mass (kneel, sit, stand, genuflect, kneel again, etc.). As an Anglican by upbringing, I've been there—bringing friends to church always involved a lot of whispered cues and helping them to maneuver the kneelers. So perhaps somewhere along the journey of owning your faith as an adult, you've felt a certain lib-eration in shedding some of these practices.

Other friends of mine raised in the evangelical or charismatic streams of the church with an underdeveloped experience of Praxis are leery of spiritual practices because, to them, they reek of a works-based righteousness. The idea of spiritual practices can trigger an automatic shame response because of difficulties dis-tinguishing between Praxis as a response to grace and Praxis as a *means* to grace. What we are aiming for is the former, but I can appreciate that it can be complex.

Richard Foster has an analogy that may help all of us to grow in our appreciation for spiritual practices while simultaneously locating their proper place in this journey of grace. He describes spiritual practices as a pathway between two chasms:

> Picture a long, narrow ridge with a sheer drop-off on either side. The chasm to the right is the way of moral bankruptcy

through human strivings for righteousness. Historically this has been called the heresy of moralism. The chasm to the left is moral bankruptcy through the absence of human strivings. This has been called the heresy of antinomianism. On the ridge there is a path, the Disciplines of the spiritual life. This path leads to the inner transformation and healing for which we seek. We must never veer off to the right or to the left, but stay on the path. The path is fraught with severe difficulties, but also with incredible joys. As we travel on this path the blessing of God will come upon us and reconstruct us into the image of Jesus Christ. We must always remember that the path does not produce the change; it only places us where the change can occur.[5]

The transformative, healing power of spiritual practices does not lie in their rote execution. On their own, spiritual practices can do nothing for us. Their power lies only in where they lead us: into the presence of the Holy Spirit. Spiritual practices don't transform us, but they do lead us to the One who can. So neither should they be mindless performative exercises that mean nothing to us, nor should they be a means of trying to earn God's love and favor. Understood and practiced with intention, spiritual practices become a conduit for intimacy and grace. Speaking to this tension, Aaron Niequist puts it this way: "Grace alone makes the River flow, but we need to wade into the water. Grace alone makes the vine grow, but we need to build the trellis. Grace alone makes the wind blow, but spiritual practices help us humbly open the window, day by day, moment by moment. The invitation is participation."[6]

The trellis image is an age-old metaphor for using spiritual practices to create an intentional way of life. Picture a beautiful arched entryway of roses into a garden, or an impressive display of roses creeping up the side of a house. They didn't grow this way by themselves; the gardener likely used some form of trellis. A trellis doesn't make roses grow. It doesn't produce the visual and olfactory glory of a mature rosebush. But it does provide the structure and support necessary for those roses to grow. Without some form of trellis—a fence, a stake, a tree, or some type of elaborate garden structure—roses tend to flop over from the weight of their vines. In the same way, a way of life built around intentional spiritual practices won't produce spiritual fruit in our lives or in the lives of our children, but it will provide the support and structure needed for this growth to occur.

THE IMPORTANCE OF A WAY OF LIFE

Picture the scene: My boys are making lunch on a Saturday. They have buttered up some fresh slices of sourdough and have filled them with generous slices of sharp cheddar. Noah confidently handles the frying pan and spatula while Silas does a little back-seat cooking: "The cheese is melting! Flip it over! Don't burn it!" After a few minutes, they each have themselves a perfectly browned, perfectly melted, delicious grilled cheese sandwich. They carry their culinary masterpieces over to the table. But before they dive in, Silas heads to the fridge, locates a jar of Gulden's Spicy Brown mustard, and they each carefully spread a thin layer of spicy goodness on top of the grilled cheese before sinking their teeth into all its cheesy glory.

This may puzzle, amuse, or disturb you—unless of course, you happen to know my family, in which case you will immediately think, "Of course. They are Cowans." This is exactly how I eat my grilled cheese, and it's exactly how my dad eats his, and it's exactly how my grandfather ate his. We are now four generations deep into this lunchtime practice. We're Cowans. It's the only grilled-cheese way we know. If you remember nothing else from this book, I hope you'll remember this: grilled cheese with spicy brown mustard on top. It will change your life.

This Cowan Way of the Grilled Cheese is two things: it is distinct, and it is compelling.

First, eating grilled cheese with mustard on top is so distinct, so peculiar, that it immediately identifies us as Cowans. No one else we know does this. In the same way, the way of Jesus in our current moment is incredibly distinct. And when I say that, please know that I do not mean the political ideologies that have come to be associated with the way of Jesus in the United States lately. I mean the ancient, global way of Jesus that Christians have been practicing for two millennia: the way of enemy-love, humility, and grace; the way of generosity, self-control, and surrender; the way of justice and peace; the way of love.

The Cowan grilled cheese way is so distinct that without proper modeling and instruction in the home, my kids never would have learned to eat grilled cheese this way in a world full of mustardless grilled cheeses. In the same way, in a world that is discipling our children to live by the values of greed, power, image, hyper-individualism, sexual freedom, cancel culture, and virtue-signaling slacktivism (I could go on), our children are unlikely to learn, without our help, to walk the beautiful but peculiar way of Jesus.

But here's the other thing: the way of grilled cheese with mustard on top is not only distinct and a little bizarre, it is also extremely compelling. It is *the. best. way.* to eat grilled cheese, hands down. (Please do me a favor. Give it a try and tell me I'm wrong.) A perfectly cooked grilled cheese with a gorgeous spicy brown mustard layer slathered on top is so compelling and delicious and satisfying that my kids, no matter where they are—at a restaurant, at a friend's house, at school—will confidently ask for mustard on top, even if no one else is doing it. They know it's just that good.

And that is how I want my kids to feel about following Jesus. I want them to know, beyond a shadow of a doubt, that the way of Jesus is just that good. I want them to know this not because we told them so or because they filled out a Sunday school sheet about it one time—or even just because "the Bible tells them so." I want them to know this because they have tasted it—because their hearts have been set aflame with love for Jesus through direct Encounter with his Spirit; because their beliefs about God, themselves, and the world have been carefully shaped by God's truth; and because their experience of living out their faith through concrete practices has been so life-giving that they would do it anywhere, even if they're the only ones.

STEAL THIS IDEA:
GRILLED CHEESE WITH MUSTARD ON TOP

Ages: all

Supplies:
- Two slices of sourdough bread
- Butter, softened
- Sharp cheddar cheese, sliced
- Gulden's Spicy Brown Mustard
- Frying pan and spatula

Instructions:
- Butter one side of each slice of bread and with buttered sides facing outward, fill the inside of the sandwich with cheese.
- Heat your frying pan on medium heat and place the sandwich in the pan.
- When the first side has browned to your liking, flip the sandwich.

- If the second side browns before the cheese has fully melted, turn the heat down to low and cover the pan.
- Place your perfectly cooked sandwich on a plate. Add a thin layer of mustard on top of the sandwich.
- Cut in half or quarters as desired and prepare for your life to change.

In the season ahead, the church—especially the evangelical church—will need to rely on Encounter and Praxis more than it ever has. Right thinking about God and the world—as critical as that is right now—will not be enough on its own to provide our children with the full-bodied intoxicating taste of God's kingdom they need right now. More than engaging their minds through Bible stories (our typical go-to discipleship move for kids), we need to focus on engaging their hearts through Encounter and their feet through Praxis. So let's look at how to make our proactive discipleship robust, multidimensional, and the basis of a distinct, compelling way of life.

UP, IN, OUT, WITH

I learned how to swim at summer camp when I was seven, and I still remember the little chant that accompanied the elementary backstroke: "Up, Out, Together, Glide!" Hands and feet follow a similar pattern—up like a chicken, out like an X, together like a pencil—ending with a nice little ergonomic glide through the water. If I were to make a chant to guide us through the discipleship journey, it would be similar: "Up, In, Out, With!" Let me explain.

At Sanctuary Church in Providence, we talk about discipleship being a journey traveled in four distinct directions.

Up: Being with Jesus. This direction leads us toward deeper intimacy with God and greater understanding of his purposes. Some classic Upward practices include worship, Scripture study, and prayer.

In: Becoming like Jesus. This direction leads us on the inner journey of becoming healed and whole people as we are "transformed into his image" more and more (2 Corinthians 3:18). Classic Inward practices include things like confession, silence, and journaling.

 Out: Doing what Jesus did. The Outward direction leads us into the world to demonstrate, in word and in deed, that Jesus is Lord. Witness, hospitality, and compassion are some examples of Outward practices.

 With: Following Jesus together. Finally, this direction leads us into community. The way of Jesus cannot be lived alone. Withward practices include gathering for worship, eating together, and celebrating.

Thinking about discipleship this way keeps it from becoming too narrow. Proactive discipleship involves creating a way of life around intentional spiritual practices. And choosing practices that help us to journey in each of these four directions will make our journey robust and complete, filling out that trellis with a full and healthy rosebush rather than a spindly little stalk.

Imagine a generation of young people—your children among them—who know what it means to be with Jesus, who have become more and more like him as they've grown, who seek to do what he did as they move through the world, and who are committed to journeying with one another. Without a doubt, this group of Jesus-followers will come across as a little bizarre as they pursue this way of life in a post-Christian world. (Whenever Harper's mom, Corrie, and I are feeling this way, we text each other: #weirdosforever.) But I think it's possible—highly likely, even—that they will also come across as undeniably, magnetically, compellingly beautiful to those who have never seen or experienced anything quite like the way of Jesus.

In the following chapters we'll talk about how to tailor spiritual practices for your child's age and faith stage and how to create an easy-to-use plan for each child and your family as a whole. But the pattern we'll use to help us create this intentional way of life will remain the same: "Up, In, Out, With!"

QUESTIONS FOR REFLECTION

1. What do you hope your kids will be like as adults? Where does following Jesus fall on your list of priorities for them? Take a moment to evaluate whether your actions today match up with your stated priorities.

2. Which stream of the church—sacramental, evangelical, or charismatic—do you most resonate with? Where do you see the impact of this stream on your own walk with Jesus and on your journey of discipling your kids?

3. How healthy is your relationship with spiritual practices? Is there any work you need to do around your posture toward spiritual practices before you introduce them to your children?

4. Which direction—Up, In, Out, With—comes most naturally to you in your own walk with Jesus? Which is the easiest for you to lead as you disciple your kids? Which is the most challenging or underrepresented direction in your life?

For pastors and church leaders

1. If you had to describe your church in terms of its stream or streams, what would you say?

2. How familiar or comfortable is your church with the concept of spiritual practices? What is your experience personally with spiritual practices?

3. Does your church have a framework for discipleship? Have you—or could you—apply that framework to discipling children?

6¾

AN INTRODUCTION TO
JOHN WESTERHOFF

I suggest that faith grows like a tree, by adding rings. Comparing faith development to tree development seems to fit, because a one-year-old tree is truly and completely a tree. As it develops, it doesn't become more truly a tree; it only becomes more complex. In the same way, one stage of faith is not better or more truly faith than another.

JOHN WESTERHOFF,
BRINGING UP CHILDREN
IN THE CHRISTIAN FAITH

MANY TIMES IN MY PARENTING JOURNEY, I have wished that kids came with owners' manuals—perhaps you can relate. For example, when Noah slept soundly in the hospital the first week of his life but began nightly three-hour screaming fits as soon as we came home, or the very stressful months when we were learning to manage Silas's asthma, or our current struggles to keep a certain child in his room at night (see my highlight reel on Instagram titled "Why is Si Awake?" if you want a good laugh[1]).

While I can't give you an owner's manual for the spiritual development of your children, what I can give you is a roadmap.

American theologian and seminary professor John Westerhoff developed a model to describe the spiritual development of children. His model identifies four distinct stages of faith and uses the imagery of tree rings to describe how each stage relates to the next. The tree ring metaphor helps us understand that faith stages are cumulative; the new stage does not progress past the previous one, leaving it behind, but rather transcends and includes it. Experiential faith is present in the Affiliative stage. Experiential and Affiliative faith are both present in the Searching stage. And all three are present in adult Owned faith.

In the next three chapters we will explore these stages in depth, along with specific spiritual practices to try with your kids in each stage.

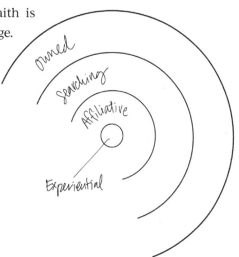

7

AGES ZERO TO SIX

The Experiential Stage (or The Blur Years)

Children have an inbuilt spirituality.
As a Christian, I believe this to be part of
what it means to be made in the image of
God. We are designed for a link with God, and
however much humanity's rebellion against
God has twisted that design, it lingers on in
us. In little children, it lingers strongly.

RON BUCKLAND,
CHILDREN AND THE GOSPEL

A TYPICAL MORNING in the life of my friend Jenna goes like this: She begins her day at 6:00 a.m., when the baby wakes up twenty minutes earlier than expected. On his way to the gym, her husband Michael plops the hungry little cherub next to Jenna in bed with an apologetic smile. Twenty minutes later, her first interaction with her two-year-old involves a distraught, high-volumed complaint about a missing can of seltzer from the day before. While getting her six-year-old ready for school—making lunch and locating the pink leggings, not the yellow ones—she discovers the dishwasher has failed to clean the dishes from the night before. It is, in fact, officially dead. After hand-washing the cereal bowls, she returns to the breakfast table to find the baby covered from a blowout. Swooping her out of the highchair, she smiles—not so apologetically—as she hands her back to Michael, arriving home that very moment from the gym. By 8:00 a.m., Jenna is ready for the nap she'll never get to take that day.

We might as well rename this stage "the blur years." The years when you can't sleep, can't finish a thought without interruption, can't shower or even pee in private, and can't leave the house without packing enough for an overnight trip. The season where the mantra "the days are long but the years are short" rings in your ears, simultaneously encouraging you and causing you anxiety. On the one hand, you're eager to arrive at the promised land of kids getting up and making their own breakfast on Saturday mornings (it's pure magic, friends); on the other hand, a little part of you wants them to stay little forever. When you are in the thick of pregnancy and sleepless nights and diapers and potty training and sleepless nights and constant colds and nap strikes—and did I mention sleepless nights?—it can be hard to imagine ever having bandwidth for something like discipleship, and it can be tempting to think they're so little it might not make that much of a difference anyway.

If this resonates with you, please know that I see you and I get it. I remember crying in the lobby of our church, having arrived for worship only to spend the majority of the service in the Nursing Mothers' Room with Noah, wondering if it was even worth it to continue trying to show up on Sunday mornings. I'll never forget what Sue—a friend with five adult children and empathy for days—said to me that morning. She pointed me to Isaiah 40:11:

> He tends his flock like a shepherd:
>   He gathers the lambs in his arms
> and carries them close to his heart;
>   he gently leads those that have young.

Sue reminded me that God was not oblivious to my limitations and exhaustion. Very much the opposite, she assured me that he was acutely aware of it and that he would lead me gently through this season. Gentleness when I had nothing left to give. Gentleness when I couldn't even pray. Gentleness when I wanted to throw things at the wall in the middle of the night (one of our children didn't sleep through the night consistently until he was four).

So please read this chapter with a gentleness for yourself that emulates the gentleness the Father has for you. You won't be able to do everything you plan for. Sometimes puke and skipped naps and fevers will derail your days. God sees it all and gets it. This same God allowed himself to become a sleepless infant, and a messy toddler, a "threenager," and a preschooler with a million questions—because he loves you. So part of your invitation is to allow that love to gently lead you during these years.

But friends, do allow the Holy Spirit to *lead* you. It may feel like the task of discipleship is impossible given your constraints or meaningless given how tiny your children are. But neither of these things are true. So from under that giant umbrella of gentleness, please allow yourself to be led and to be challenged. You will meet God in your parenting more than you ever thought possible during this stage.

In the Experiential stage, the primary mode of spiritual engagement is experience rather than a cognitive understanding of

Experiential

faith. Children in this stage learn by doing, and they discover what to do by imitating those closest to them. Following Jesus in the Experiential stage centers on participating in the practices and rituals of faith by engaging the body and the senses in discipleship.

My own children learned to participate in corporate prayer and worship before they ever understood what they were saying or singing. When he was just learning to talk, Noah would "pray" at mealtimes by saying "A-wuzza-wuzza-wuzza-wuzza-wuzza. . . . *Amen!*" And I have a video of Silas, at age three, reciting the Lord's Prayer. He's spot on with every single word through the beginning but as he rounds the corner into "but deliver us from evil" the words all meld together in adorable gibberish until, practically out of breath, he excitedly gets to the "Amen!" like he's stumbled across some kind of finish line.

My friend Cory told me that his three-year-old presents every boo-boo to him for prayer, because "he sees me doing that, and he wants to be like Dad." Cory explained that he and his wife "grew up being taught to sing cultural songs and kiss their cuts to make kids feel better. We decided that we wanted to teach Jael to look at God whenever in need, even for little cuts. In order for him to embrace it, we practiced it with each other. We would just pray for each other when we had headaches, stubbed our toe, and even just had coughs. He picked up on that so fast, and now it's a part of who he is."[1]

On the surface level, these anecdotes may seem spiritually meaningless, but I believe they are full of weight and significance. When I see little children imitating the actions of their believing parents, I see God's constant, gracious movement toward humanity—in this case, moving toward these little ones through the habits of their parents. I see a God who uses the experiences and actions of embodied faith like stable, secure handholds to grasp onto, much like the eager fingers we parents extend as these same babies learn to walk.

Stories, songs, memorized verses and prayers, rituals such as bedtime prayers and praying before meals, and familiar rhythms like Sunday worship—these embodied practices help the child to learn what following Jesus is like. Later on, as their minds mature, they will be able to interpret and understand these experiences in a new way, but this does not diminish the reality that, to these little ones, these embodied experiences are an expression of genuine faith.

BABIES AND TODDLERS

It's tempting to think there's no discipleship to be done when our kids seem like little more than eating, crying, sleeping, pooping bundles of cuteness. But I remember being completely arrested one day by the Holy Spirit while rocking and praying for baby Noah. My typical prayer at that time was that Noah would grow up to know God. In that moment, I suddenly felt convicted that my prayer was too small. Instead, I sensed the Holy Spirit inviting me to pray that Noah would know God *now*, that he would be distinctly aware of God's presence and love and power, even right there in my arms.

That perspective shift changed me. I began to trust God's ability and desire to engage my child more than I had in the past and to think about this preverbal time as an important season to shape and form the habits that would eventually shape and form our family life. Like laying train tracks or building a foundation, our intentionality during the months of infancy and toddlerhood is far from spiritually irrelevant. My friend Andrew talks about praying prayers his babies didn't understand and reading them Bible stories they couldn't comprehend as a way of shaping and forming himself as a Christian parent. And I believe these practices will shape the child as well in ways we can't see or comprehend. Few people I know question whether they should read bedtime stories to their preverbal children or talk to them in fully formed sentences. Similarly, praying with our babies, worshiping, reading them stories about Jesus, and inviting the Holy Spirit's presence and blessing—none of this intentionality is wasted.

Another thing to remember about the Experiential stage is that, for our littlest ones, we parents and caretakers are the primary model for what God is like. For example, the idea that "Jesus loves us" is only understood via the child's reference point for "love." At this age, this reference point is not some abstract theory of love but the experience of being loved by *you*. The more you can help your children associate your love with God's love—because, in fact, yours is quite literally designed to point them to his—the more they will know, beyond human cognition, that "God is love" (1 John 4:8).

For example, one thing Greg and I began doing when the boys were toddlers was allowing them to be held during worship rather than making them sit still or stand in the pew. As challenging as it was to abandon the concept of personal space, especially during humid Rhode Island summers in our non-air-conditioned church building, Greg and I were committed to encouraging their instinct to cuddle and be close as a way of helping them associate worship with love. Eventually this became a routine. We chose not to drop them off at the nursery at the beginning of the service but to wait until the sermon began, so they could be present for worship and enjoy some cuddle time. We liked to imagine that, in some small way, they were experiencing what it felt like to be held by God. Now that they are older and too big to be held, I still try (unless rebuffed, but I'm usually not) to put an arm around them, or a hand on their shoulder, or to give a little back scratch while we sing.

STEAL THIS IDEA:
WORSHIP CUDDLES

Ages: babies, toddlers, preschoolers

Instructions:

- Allow very young children to remain with you during worship. Consider dropping them off at the nursery or child-care only during the quiet parts of the service such as the sermon and prayer times.

- Obviously don't force it, but if your children will allow you to hold them, go ahead and pick them up and keep them close as you sing. You may find a baby carrier helpful. Piggyback is a great option for older kids.

- Whisper in their ear how much you love them, how much Jesus loves them, and the basic meaning of the song. "This song is about how wonderful God is."

- Help them to sing along or even to raise their hands in worship to "hug" God.

PRESCHOOLERS

As your kids become more verbal, with attention spans increasing slightly, this is a great time to begin inviting them to participate in verbal practices around prayer and Scripture.

As soon as our boys were old enough to answer emotions questions, around age two or three, we began a daily bedtime prayer of examen, an ancient spiritual practice of looking back on the day to reflect on where you noticed God's presence and where you may have missed it. One of the fruits of a regular practice of examen is learning to recognize God's presence with you at all times, through the moments of consolation (joy, hope, awareness of God) as well as desolation (pain, despair, or feeling distant from God). Since the idea of "noticing God's presence" is a bit beyond a three-year-old's ability to engage, we simplified the questions to these:

- When were you happy today? (Everyone answers, including parents.)

- When were you sad today? (Everyone answers, including parents.)

- Who was with you when you were happy and when you were sad? (Child answers, "Jesus!")

Too often, in the (White) Western church, especially, an underdeveloped theology of suffering can mean that one's first experience of suffering quickly leads to questioning God's presence or goodness. Concerned about this dynamic, I wanted my kids to know deeply in their spiritual bones that God is with them always. He's with them in times of great joy and in times of great suffering. I wanted this to be such a foundational truth that it would carry them through any future suffering in their life with the confidence that God had not abandoned them.

I realized just how deeply this truth had anchored itself in Noah's soul when he was preparing to visit the dentist for the first time at age three and was very nervous about it. We kept reassuring him that they were only going to count his teeth this time, maybe brush them a little, that I would be able to stay with him in the exam room, and that nothing was going to hurt. This conversation went on for days. At one point, feeling a little exasperated and hoping to remind Noah that I would be right there in the room with him, I asked, "But buddy, who is going to be *with* you at the dentist?" He sighed with visible relief and said, "Ohhhh. Jesus." I had to stifle a laugh, but I realized in that moment that Jesus' presence was actually more reassuring to him than mine, and that was just fine with me.

On a less elevated note, another time when I was feeling particularly frustrated with Silas, I blurted out, "Silas Johnson, what is *with* you?!" Without skipping a beat, he looked at me with a coy smile and said, "Jesus!" In an instant all my frustration melted into uncontrollable laughter.

When the boys were a bit older, we changed the bedtime questions to the more classic examen questions about noticing and missing God's presence. Growing up, my parents used to do a version of this weekly at the dinner table with us, calling it a "God hunt." A God hunt is similar to a bear hunt, but in this case you are not hunting for furry animals but hunting for God sightings throughout the day or week.

STEAL THIS IDEA: BEDTIME EXAMEN

Ages: preschoolers and up

Instructions:

- At bedtime, invite your child or children to think back over the day, and ask, "When were you happy today?" and "When were you sad today?"
  - Let them answer. Don't suggest or correct.
  - Share when you felt happy and sad today.
- Then ask, "Who was with you today when you were happy and when you were sad?"
  - Help them learn to answer, "Jesus!"
- Close the time by thanking Jesus that he is always with us, no matter what.

STEAL THIS IDEA: GOD HUNT

Ages: verbal kids

Instructions:

- Choose a time when all family members are present and distractions are limited. Dinnertime or bedtime often work well.
- Explain, "We are going on a God hunt—we are looking for where we saw God today or this week. God can be found in so many places if we learn to look for him."

- Have each family member share where they saw God that day. Maybe it was in a moment of joy, peace, love, beauty, or kindness. Maybe it was in a difficult moment that was made bearable by his comfort.
- If your children struggle to find God in their day, other family members can "hunt" with them. Rest assured; he was there.
- Close the time by thanking God that he is always with us.

Older toddlers and preschoolers can also begin memorizing Scripture. Though they may not fully comprehend the words they are saying at first, the idea is to help our children "hide God's word in their hearts" (see Psalm 119:11), internalizing deep truths about God that go beyond surface-level comprehension to heart-level knowledge and assurance.

My number-one suggestion here is to translate Scripture into language and ideas that little ones can understand. My favorite example of this, from my own childhood, was a translation of 1 Peter 5:7 which says, "Cast all your anxiety on him because he cares for you." My mom's version for us was "Throw it to Jesus." Whenever we were worried, Mom would say, "Throw it to Jesus!" I still use this phrase today—and still believe Jesus can handle the worst I throw at him. This idea was hidden in my heart in childhood in a way that has continued to bear fruit in my life as an adult.

Here are some others that Greg and I have used over the years with our kids:

- Psalm 4:8: "In peace I will lie down and sleep, for you alone, LORD, make me dwell in safety."

  Little Kid Version: "I will close my eyes and go to sleep because God makes me so so so so safe."

- Ephesians 4:26: "In your anger, do not sin."

  Little Kid Version: "When you're mad, do not hit, bite, kick, throw things, scream . . ."

- 2 Corinthians 10:5: "We demolish arguments and every pretension that sets itself up against the knowledge of God, and we take captive every thought to make it obedient to Christ."

  Little Kid Version: "Does that sound like something Jesus would say? Let's send that yucky thought to jail."

You will be amazed at what your kids are capable of memorizing from a very young age. And please keep in mind that you are not the only one discipling your kids. The world around them—from the shows they watch to the songs they hear on the radio to the things they learn about in school—is not neutral when it comes to their formation. The world is actively discipling them in gospels of its own: the gospel of fashion, the gospel of greed, the gospel of individualism, the gospel of sexual liberty, even the gospel of nationalism. I remember when Noah came home from kindergarten one day and recited the Pledge of Allegiance perfectly to me. I honestly had not even considered that he was capable of memorizing something that substantial and, like a punch in the gut, I realized that his teachers were doing a better job discipling him than I was. I feel very strongly that, as Jesus-followers, our primary allegiance needs to be given to King Jesus above and before any secondary allegiances we make. So I found it troubling that this pledge of secondary allegiance was hidden in his heart before I had been intentional about helping him hide even the Lord's Prayer there.

It was a wake-up call for us. Greg, being the church history nerd that he is, began to take the boys on walks to memorize Luther's go-to mini-catechism: referred to as Luther's "Little Dagger," this teaching tool comprises very simply the Ten Commandments, the Lord's Prayer, and the Apostles' Creed (a basic statement of Christian faith). Now you absolutely do not need to steal that idea, but I do encourage you to consider what messages, what gospels, and what allegiances are being hidden in your kids' hearts, even at this tender age—and what truths you want to help them hide there as well.

One easy way to encourage Scripture memorization is through song, and it is nearly effortless on your part—you can disciple your kids during playtime or in the car or while you are doing something else entirely.[2] Music is an incredibly helpful memorization tool. To this day, I still hum the books of the Bible song I learned when I was seven, whenever I'm looking up a verse.

Eventually, as they grow, it will be important to help our kids understand the things they have committed to memory. Memorization without comprehension will not serve them particularly well in the long run. But just like my understanding of what it means to "throw it to Jesus" has matured, we can absolutely help our kids grow into age-appropriate understanding of what has been hidden in their hearts.

EARLY ELEMENTARY SCHOOL

For five- and six-year-olds heading off to school, you can begin to take advantage of some of the routines that come with a more structured school day as well as their growing ability to read and write.

When my sister and I were in elementary school, my parents began a daily morning prayer routine with us. Right after breakfast and before the school bus came, we would gather in Mom's study for about ten minutes of prayer as a family. Our routine was very simple: we would pray for immediate requests and prayer needs, then spend some time praying generally for friends and family, and finish with the Lord's Prayer. Our black labs, Tara and Tika, became so accustomed to our mad dash for the school bus after morning prayer that anytime anyone prayed in our home, the dogs would excitedly jump to their feet at the word *amen*.

To hold our attention and help us to participate fully in this prayer time, Mom created what she called a "Prayer Tree," a giant bare tree cut out of brown posterboard that she taped to the side of her filing cabinet. She cut out cardstock leaves, placed them in a box on her coffee table, and invited us to write prayer requests on the leaves, along with the date. The only rule was that the requests needed to be specific and measurable enough to easily determine when they had been answered. For example, "world peace" was not something you should put on a leaf, but "an end to the Gulf War" was on a leaf for thirteen months from January 1990 to February 1991.

Other things that went on leaves over the years: prayers for friends and family battling illnesses; for help with various school assignments, tests, and other sources of childhood anxiety; for the healing of a family member's marriage that was in trouble; for friends to come to know Jesus; for safe travels during various trips; for world events like wars and famine. Each day, we would "deal" out the leaves much like cards until the box was empty, and we would pray for whatever ended up in our hand. Whenever a prayer was answered with a yes, it would be taped up on the tree. I distinctly remember the sense of joy and satisfaction every time we taped a new leaf up and loved watching the branches fill up with leaves throughout the year.

One leaf I will never forget had the name "Terry Waite" on it. In 1987, when I was six, Terry Waite, an experienced hostage negotiator and assistant to the Archbishop of Canterbury, was kidnapped in Beirut, Lebanon. Terry was in Lebanon as an official representative of the Church of England, negotiating for the release of four hostages being held by the Islamic Jihad Organization. While in discussions with the organization, he was promised safe conduct to visit the hostages but was double-crossed and taken hostage himself. We added Terry's name to a leaf, as well as each of the other hostages, and prayed daily for their release. Terry was released on November 18, 1991, and that tattered and creased leaf finally went up on the tree. Later, we mailed the leaf to him with a letter explaining our daily prayers for his release.

When prayers were answered with a no, they were taped to the cabinet near the bottom of the tree, like fallen leaves lying on the ground. But there were far fewer of those, and I honestly don't remember any of them in detail. Mom often reminded us about how she began this practice with a gnawing fear of having to explain unanswered prayer to us—a fear that was met with the resounding visual of a tree full of leaves year after year after year. I do remember praying for two people who eventually died: we prayed for three months for my grandmother to be healed after an asthma-related brain injury, which eventually resulted in her death, and we prayed for the healing of a dear friend from colon cancer, which also resulted in her death. Instead of taping these leaves on the ground, we taped them up above the tree to symbolize our hope that they were now with Jesus.

Each Thanksgiving, we removed the leaves and read them aloud at the dinner table, thanking God for each very specific answered prayer. The influence on my life from this daily practice was profound. Though I do remember feeling angry at God when my grandmother died, the lasting lesson I've carried with me from years of childhood intercessory prayer was not that sometimes God answers with a no—which is true and I surely experienced—but that when you pray, God listens and things in our world—from spelling tests to marriages to wars—change.

In addition to immediate and specific prayer requests, my parents also helped us to pray general prayers of blessing for family and loved ones. Each year we collected all the Christmas card photos we received from friends and family and added them to the prayer box, replacing last year's photos when necessary. During our morning prayer times, each of us would be given one photo card along with our handful of leaves. We learned how to pray not only for people we loved dearly but also for people we barely knew. We prayed for InterVarsity presidents and Episcopal bishops, college friends of my parents, overseas missionaries, and people we'd never meet in real life. We learned how to pray that they would experience God's presence and joy, and we even learned to listen to God for specific things to pray for.

When I was six, I announced during one of these prayer times that my godmother, who we knew was pregnant but hadn't reached her due date yet, had just given birth. I confidently announced that she'd had a boy and had named him Joseph. Mom called her friend up a little hesitantly later that day and discovered that yes, in fact, Joseph had been born that very day.

STEAL THIS IDEA: PRAYER TREE

Ages: elementary school (readers)

Supplies:

- A bare "tree" somewhere visible in the home (You could cut a trunk and branches out of paper or posterboard and tape to a wall; paint a mural on a blank wall; or trim a tree branch, remove the leaves, and set it up somewhere inside)
- A collection of "leaves" cut out of thick paper or cardstock (Material should be easy to write on and durable enough to be handled repeatedly)
- A container for the leaves and/or photos
- Pens
- Tape
- Christmas card photos (optional)

Instructions:

- Invite family members to write prayer requests on the leaves. Requests should be as specific and time-bound as possible (e.g., "that John is healed of cancer" rather than "world peace").
- Spend time daily or weekly interceding for the requests. Pass out the leaves to each family member and invite everyone to pray for their leaves. If using Christmas card photos, pass out one photo to each person and invite general prayers for those pictured.
- As prayers are answered, attach them to the tree. Do not be afraid that none will be answered—wait and see!
- There are times when God does not answer our prayers the way we have asked—most poignantly when prayers for healing are not answered or when someone we love dies. When this happens, you may be tempted to over-explain and "cover" for God as you wrestle yourself with the reality of unanswered prayer. Instead, I encourage you to see this as an opportunity to teach your children about the practice known as "lament." This is when we simply cry out to God in our pain, confident that his heart breaks as well. You can reassure your little ones that God is never the author of suffering and that he is sad too. He is also working to fix everything that is broken, and we can look forward to the day when "'He will wipe every tear from [our] eyes. There will be no more death' or mourning or crying or pain" (Revelation 21:4).
- At Thanksgiving, remove all the leaves from the tree and read them aloud, giving thanks for each answered prayer throughout the year.

The bottom line for little ones is this: help them to do what you're doing as you follow Jesus. Engage their senses and their full bodies. Use ritual and repeated practices. In all your interactions, help them to associate God with love and love with God. Westerhoff puts it this way:

> For Christian faith, word and deed are never separated. Experienced faith, therefore, results from our interactions with other faithing selves. And thus the question for a parent to ask is this: What is it to be Christian with my child? To seriously address that question is to discover what sort of environments, experiences, and interactions are necessary for our own and another's life in faith. To live with others in Christian ways, to put our words into deeds and our deeds into words, to share life with another, to be open to influence as well as to influence, and to interact with other faithing selves in a community of Christian faith is to provide the necessary environment for Experienced faith.[3]

EXPERIENTIAL STAGE PRACTICES

Up: Being with Jesus.

- Pray a "Jesus, help" prayer for everything from lost toys to scraped knees to monsters.

- Memorize the Lord's Prayer.

- Anoint with oil when sick.

- Pray spiritual warfare prayers: "Go away, monsters, in the name of Jesus."

- Pray in tongues with or over your child.

- Play a thank-you game: How many things can you think of to thank God for?

- Use toddler versions of memory verses:

  - When anxious: "Throw it to Jesus" (see 1 Peter 5:7)

- With trouble sleeping: "I will close my eyes and go to sleep because God makes me so so so so safe." (see Psalm 4:8)
- For aggressive behavior: "When you're mad, do not bite." (see Ephesians 4:26)

- Read or retell Bible stories.

- Have a dance party to worship music or "Jesus music."

- Incorporate worship cuddles.

- Whisper "translations" of song lyrics in your child's ear during worship at church to help them understand what the song is about.

In: Becoming like Jesus.

- Share daily "gratefuls and grumbles" as a family at dinner or bedtime. This is essentially like the bedtime examen above, but with language that little kids can easily identify with.

- Practice an apology and reconciliation liturgy: "I'm sorry for X," with the response, "I love you and I forgive you."

- Identify and name emotions, then match emotions to Scripture:

  - It's okay that you're sad. Jesus cried too (see John 11:35).

  - It's okay that you're mad. Jesus got mad too (see Matthew 21). But, when we are mad, we don't hit, bite, kick, scream (see Ephesians 4:26).

  - When I am afraid, I will trust God (see Psalm 56:3).

  - When I'm worried, I can throw it to Jesus (see 1 Peter 5:7).

Out: Doing what Jesus did.

- Kids love to "help." At church outreach events, give them kid-sized tasks (stacking things, picking up trash, etc.).

- Do neighborhood trash pickup.

- Pray for friends who don't know Jesus. Explain: Did you know that not everyone knows Jesus? How does that make you feel? How do you think they could hear about him?

- If you provide a weekly allowance, let them put a tithe of their own in the offering plate.

- Pray for any sirens (ambulance, police, fire) you hear or see.

- Pray for people asking for money, engage them, or both.

- Pray for and write to missionaries.

With: Following Jesus together.

- Attend worship regularly as a family.

- Teach kids that "church" is not a building or an event but a bigger family they belong to.

- Let toddlers participate in adult worship. Don't automatically rush them to the nursery if you can help it.

- Allow young children to serve alongside parents at church—handing out bulletins, picking up trash, etc.

- Practice a regular "extended family dinner" weekly or monthly. Cultivate the expectation that others are welcomed at your table regularly. Model and practice hospitality.

- Explain the defining values of the family: "We don't X. We do Y, because Jesus does Y."

- Practice sabbath with family playtime together every week. No work, no phones, everyone present.

- Create annual rhythms such as family camp.

QUESTIONS FOR REFLECTION

1. Spend a few minutes thinking about any of your children currently in this stage. Acknowledge and thank God for the faith you see growing and developing in them. What do you appreciate most about how they relate to God?

2. What are your favorite things about this stage? What do you enjoy the most about this stage as you parent? What things about this stage can make discipleship enjoyable or fun?

3. What are the challenges of this stage? What are your least favorite aspects of parenting through this stage? What about this stage can make discipleship challenging?

4. Each of Westerhoff's stages is present in adult, Owned faith. Take a moment to evaluate how Experiential faith has shaped your own spiritual journey: What have been your most compelling experiences of God lately? What is your current relationship with ritual and spiritual routine like? In what ways do your spiritual practices engage your body and your senses?

5. What is one new practice you'd like to try with your Experiential-aged child?

For pastors and church leaders

1. How would you describe your church's ministry to Experiential-aged kids? How does your programming encourage the "believing by doing" mindset?

2. How are you supporting parents of Experiential-aged kids?

8

AGES SEVEN TO ELEVEN

The Affiliative Stage (or The Squad Years)

> *Family is the one human institution we have no*
> *choice over. We get in simply by being born, and*
> *as a result we are involuntarily thrown together*
> *with a menagerie of strange and unlike people.*
> *Church calls for another step: to voluntarily*
> *choose to band together with a strange menagerie*
> *because of a common bond in Jesus Christ. I have*
> *found that such a community more resembles*
> *a family than any other human institution.*

PHILIP YANCEY, *CHURCH: WHY BOTHER?*
MY PERSONAL PILGRIMAGE

EVERY THURSDAY NIGHT in the Jewelry District of Providence, thirteen little girls scoot their folding chairs into a circle for Sanctuary Church's Girls' Bible Study. Designed for first to third graders and led by parents, this space is contributing to a shift in how we think about children's ministry at our church.[1]

One mom said her daughter is feeling "such camaraderie and friendship and love toward these girls. She doesn't necessarily put her finger on the fact that 'these kids all believe the same thing as me,' but she's starting to notice that there is a difference between these girls and the kids she hangs out with at school. I want Juniper to feel more like the kids who love Jesus than the kids who don't. And I think that's where the Girls' Bible Study comes in, because she really feels this special place of belonging there."[2]

Emilia, a first-grader, said this: "When you're with your friends, and you're with God too, and your whole family, it makes you happier and satisfied. You just want to stay with your friends forever and you don't want to leave."[3] And Elsie, also a first-grader, loves Girls' Bible Study so much that her mom recently found her surrounded by a circle of teddy bears, leading a Bible study for them.[4]

These anecdotes perfectly illustrate the primary mode of spiritual engagement for this stage: belonging to a community. In this stage, the child begins to personally identify with the faith community and finds great meaning and joy in belonging to the group. You can see this in Emilia's description: she loves being with her friends, *and* God, *and* her family. You can also see it reflected in Elsie's teddy bear Bible study: not only has she experienced a spiritual "tribe," she's re-creating it for her babies. Westerhoff says of this stage: "All of us need to feel that we belong to a self-conscious community and that through our active participation can make a contribution to its life. . . . Of crucial importance is the sense that we are wanted, needed, accepted, and important to the community."[5]

In this stage, children continue to imitate the parents' spiritual behavior but no longer out of pure instinct. They grow in their desire to be like Mom and Dad and to be part of the group in their own right. At the beginning of this stage, the primary sense of belonging is to the family, but near the end of this stage, the peer group becomes more and more significant.

While parents talking about and practicing their faith in the home continues to be the most influential factor in the child's spiritual development, the Withward direction becomes extremely important for this age group precisely because of their interest in belonging. This stage is a time to help the child connect beyond the family to the church—both to believing adults and to spiritual peers.

CONNECTING WITH OTHER BELIEVING ADULTS

My dad, known to my boys as Papi, has been doing "Papi Bible Study" with each of my boys, independently, since they were in kindergarten. Noah is now twelve and this rhythm has been an essential part of his spiritual growth through the Affiliative stage. In person when possible, and via video chat when not, my dad has been taking him through a curriculum of his own design which has included Bible studies, biographies of saints throughout church history, and many a Bible Project video.[6] He will sometimes give us a heads up on tough topics, but mostly this space is completely independent from us.

The Sticky Faith researchers at the Fuller Youth Institute suggest that having five other Christian adults involved in the child's life is another significant factor in helping them develop a faith that sticks into adulthood.[7] These could be Sunday school teachers, godparents, your own friends, or church staff. Papi is one of our "five." It's been important for Noah as he's moved through the Affiliative stage to understand that his community of faith extends far beyond our nuclear family and local church. He has expressed this appreciation in his own words over and over again whenever he writes Papi a birthday or Christmas card: "I'm so glad you're in my life. You're such an awesome grandfather. Thank you for teaching me about Jesus." For Noah, and we anticipate for Silas as he grows, one of the key dimensions of his relationship with his grandfather is spiritual. Their deep bond is not just because they are Cowans; it's also because they are fellow Jesus-followers.

STEAL THIS IDEA: PAPI BIBLE STUDY

Ages: elementary school and up

Supplies:

- A trusted grandparent, grandparent-figure, or any trusted adult who feels like "family"
- Thirty to sixty minutes of uninterrupted time in person or via video chat

Instructions:

- Identify your "five." Who are the trusted Jesus-followers in your kids' lives who feel like family? Maybe they are, in fact, family—your parents, your siblings, a cousin—or maybe it's a Sunday school teacher, a godparent, a close friend of yours, or even a babysitter who loves Jesus and already has lots of uninterrupted time with your kids.
- Invite one of your five to do their own version of a Papi Bible Study. It doesn't need to be nearly as intense as ours—perhaps a four-week devotional during the summer, a monthly Bible Project video viewing, or a weekly check-in to share highs and lows and pray together. The point is simply to extend the child's sense of spiritual affiliation—"I believe because we believe"—beyond the nuclear family.
- For the adults who don't already have regular in-person time with your kids, video chat makes the ask relatively painless. All it takes is thirty to sixty minutes of their time from the comfort of their home or office.

CONNECTING WITH BELIEVING PEERS

As the child grows and matures, their primary sense of belonging will shift from family to peers, so helping your kids to foster meaningful friendships within the faith community is important. Many youth groups start in middle school, but I believe that starting youth-group-like experiences earlier, ones more intentionally connected to the nuclear family, might be the single best thing we could do for our Affiliative stage kiddos.

The Girls' Bible Study is one example. Another example, one of the most unexpected and beautiful outcomes of the 2020 pandemic for us, was what came to be known as the PreTeen Boy Squad (PTBS).[8]

When the pandemic hit, Greg and I talked about how to keep our boys spiritually engaged during lockdown. Papi Bible Study on video every week was an important piece of that. But, based on our knowledge of Westerhoff's stages, we knew how important maintaining connections with friends in the wider church community would be for Noah in particular. So we threw out an invitation to the parents of seven ten-year-old boys in the Sanctuary family: Would any of their boys be interested in joining Greg every other week via video chat for a forty-five-minute Bible study, followed by (with parent approval) some unsupervised hangout time? All of them said yes.

Two years later, PTBS is still going strong and was part of the inspiration for the Girls' Bible Study. We have added a "side parent" (the boys' term) each week to assist Greg with video logistics and wrangling. (Word to the wise, if you ever decide to share a Zoom whiteboard with a group of preteen boys, make sure you disable the participant editing feature. #whoops.) But the not-so-secret side goal of involving other parents was to allow them to experience the joy of watching their boys engage the Scriptures together. PTBS has been as much a discipleship tool for the parents (affectionately called the "Parent Squad") as it has been for the boys. We have done service projects together, taken family hikes, and even pulled off an optional sex-ed night with the dads. PTBS was the highlight of "church" for me during the long months of digital worship gatherings.

The magic of PTBS has been three-fold. First, because of the strong parent involvement from the beginning combined with the full blessing and support of church leadership, it has felt like something of a Venn diagram between the nuclear family and the local church.

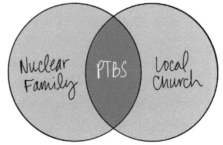

The Parent Squad worked out the curriculum together, planned the sex-ed night, and routinely participates in the study itself. Far from feeling like a burden or "my week to volunteer" when I'm on the calendar to serve as side parent, it's the highlight of my week. And other parents consistently give the same feedback. (The other consistent feedback is that everyone wishes they'd had a sex-ed night at church when they were kids.)

PTBS is also fully supported by our local church, which has a vision to see the congregation get in the game, with pastors and staff acting more like the coaches and cheerleaders than the primary players on the field. This is exactly what has happened with the PreTeen Boy Squad. Sanctuary's posture toward this expression of the church's ministry has been, "What do you need? How can we support you? We believe in you—keep going!" Part of what has made this little ecosystem flourish is the church's posture of equipping, releasing, and blessing ordinary parents to get in the game rather than staffing it up with "professionals."

The second part of the magic has been the Bible study itself. Greg is leading the boys through what's called an "inductive" Bible study, much like he does with college students in his work with InterVarsity. And they love it. The hallmark of inductive study is seeking to approach the text more like a detective looking for clues than a prosecutor trying to prove a theory deductively. There are no handouts or flashy videos or silly props or games. They read the Scripture passage together, notice little details in the text, ask good questions, and apply it to their lives with Greg's help. A huge part of PTBS's success has been believing that ten- and eleven-year-olds can handle so much more depth than what you tend to find in a typical Sunday school lesson.

Third, about six months into this experiment we decided we would start building the curriculum around Sanctuary's discipleship directions—Up, In, Out, and With. We gathered the Parent Squad, shared a Google doc with them, and began brainstorming what we could do in that space to lead our kids Upward, Inward, Outward, and Withward. Here are a few of the things the boys have done over the past six months or so, with an accompanying Scripture study to reinforce the practice:

- Up: learned how to keep a prayer journal (Exodus 33:7-11)

- In: learned how to confess their sin and to receive God's grace (John 8:1-11)

- Out: collected toiletries and other items for the refugee community in Providence (Matthew 25:35-40)

- With: committed to being friends who check in on each other, pray for each other, and love each other through thick and thin (1 Samuel 23:15-18)

Sometimes your kids will struggle to find peers like this in their own local church community. One parent I spoke with, raising teenage daughters in New York City, told me that being intentional about raising kids in the way of Jesus would not only make them "weird" by the world's standards, but also quite likely by the local church's standards as well.

STEAL THIS IDEA:
PRETEEN BOY (OR GIRL) SQUAD

Ages: preteens

Supplies:

- At least two preteens and their parents
- Thirty to sixty minutes of uninterrupted time for a video call (You could also attempt to do this in person but note that it will increase the time commitment and logistical complexity significantly)
- A lead parent and a side parent per session
- A simple plan for a Bible study and accompanying practices

Instructions:

- Find a couple like-minded parents with kids your age. Share this idea with them. Pray about it together.
- Ask your church to pray for you and support you.
- Give it a try! Aim for thirty minutes of content and thirty minutes of "hang time" at the end (with parent permission).
- Don't try to shoot the moon. Commit to meeting four times and see how it's going. If it's not working, it's fine to let it be a stand-alone experience. If it's working, keep going!

For me, a pastor's kid in a smallish church with a very small youth program, I rarely felt spiritually "normal" among a group of peers. In my predominantly Catholic town, being a pastor's kid was doubly weird—not only was I different for being "super religious," but no one had ever heard of a married priest. The most common follow-up question was "Wait, is your mom a nun?!" It wasn't all that much better at church, either. Sunday school teachers unknowingly embarrassed me by asking me not to answer (to "give the other kids a chance"), and church friends sometimes teased me for being a "goody two-shoes."

I remember talking to my parents about this when I was in fifth grade, frustrated that I never quite fit in and bemoaning the fact that because Dad was a pastor, we had to be "super religious." And I'll never forget the correction my dad made there. "Sarah," he said, "please don't misunderstand. We've made choices for our family about the kinds of spiritual habits and practices we keep not because I'm a *pastor*—but because we are Jesus-followers." It was one of those conversations that stayed with me because of how surprising it was. I had always assumed we were different— "super religious"—because it was kind of Dad's job to be that way. But my parents made sure I knew these were choices they would have made for our family no matter what.

All of this changed for me in 1992. That was the summer we first attended InterVarsity's Family Camp at Cedar Campus, located in Michigan's Upper Peninsula. When I went to the kids' program, instead of people goofing off and making fun of the content, I found a thoroughly engaging Bible discussion, passionate prayer times, and emotional worship nights around the fire. I was amazed. It seemed like every kid there was "super religious," just like me— because every family was just as serious about walking the way of Jesus as mine was. I was no longer the only one in the room who read my Bible and kept a prayer journal. I made friends that week who wrote to me all year, encouraged me to stay close to Jesus, prayed for me, and sent me Christian mixtapes. Betsy and I begged Mom and Dad to go back the following year. We ended up returning every year until I went to college.

I was eleven that summer, and knowing what I know now about Westerhoff's stages, my experience makes complete sense. It was deeply significant for me to connect with a group of peers as interested in Jesus as I was; in fact, it was life changing. And none of those people lived anywhere near me. We stayed connected all year through letters and phone calls. Just think of the kind of connections our kids could maintain today with their own cross-country friends.

STEAL THIS IDEA: CAMP!

Ages: elementary school and up

Supplies:

- An awesome Christian camp
- Sleeping bag, flashlight, bug spray, several pairs of underwear

Instructions:

- Get your kids to camp! There are so many wonderful family camps across the country. I am admittedly partial to InterVarsity and Covenant Camps (my denomination), but anywhere that will encourage you to follow Jesus as a family gets a gold star in my book!
- Also, overnight summer camps often afford kids the same kind of opportunity I experienced when I was eleven, to be around peers who are as serious about Jesus as they are. In the age of helicopter parenting, this can be tough. The first time I sent eight-year-old Noah to Camp Squanto at Pilgrim Pines in New Hampshire, the silence was deafening. I realized that every other time we'd been apart, I'd had easy access to someone with a phone for updates if I wanted them. Needless to say, the experience was good for both of us.

CULTIVATING AFFECTION FOR JESUS

While children in this stage are beginning to grow in their cognitive and intellectual abilities, Westerhoff notes that religious affections are still dominant in the Affiliative stage. He warns that we often move past affection too quickly, in favor of thinking- and belief-based spirituality:

> We have become too concerned too early with the activities of thinking in Christian education, and we forget that the intuitional mode of consciousness is of equal importance

with the intellectual. Indeed, in terms of faith, actions in the realm of the affections are prior to acts of thinking, which is why participation in the arts—drama, music, dance, sculpture, painting, and storytelling—are essential to faith. We need opportunities to act in ways that enhance the religious affections. Opportunities for experiencing awe, wonder, and mystery, as well as chances to sing, dance, paint, and act, are needed by us all.[9]

As your child grows, and even as they begin to ask intellectual questions about the journey of faith, don't forget to continue to foster and nourish their affection for Jesus. What they believe about Jesus is of critical importance. But so is what they *feel* about him. In the same way that cuddling during worship creates a feeling of safety and love for a toddler, cultivating a discipleship environment of wonder, joy, delight, creativity, and beauty for the older child will capture the heart of your nine-year-old who loves to dance, or your ten-year-old who loves to play the drums, or your seven-year-old who loves to create elaborate single-act plays. Here are some questions to ask yourself about the ways your Affiliative-aged child interacts with God:

- Do we laugh when we talk about God? Does my child know that God is fun?

- Do we sing, dance, draw, play music, or otherwise create? Does my child know that God is beautiful and creative?

- Do we play, imagine, and freely express our emotions? Does my child know that God is infinitely interesting and also infinitely interested in them?

My godson Jude experienced what his dad called "revival in a ten-year-old" that began with an increased sense of affection for Jesus, much like what I've just described. While watching season one of *The Chosen*, a series that depicts the life of Jesus and his disciples, Jude was instantly drawn to the Jesus character. One night in particular, he began to describe how much happier he got when Jesus showed up in the scenes, how much he loved Jesus, and even went to bed talking about his love for Jesus. His dad explained how over the next twenty-four hours he witnessed answers to specific prayers he'd prayed for Jude regarding his relationship with Jesus.

First, Jude began to call out to Jesus independently in prayer. Feeling anxious about something, Jude told his dad, "Remember from *The Chosen*, when Jesus was in the woods, and he was calling out to his Father (God)? Well, that's what I did tonight, I called out to Jesus and asked him to help me with my scaredness tonight." Next, he began to become curious about the spiritual lives of the most important people in his life. He asked a family member on the phone if she believed in Jesus and if they could begin praying together. Then, using a blessing that his dad prays over him each day, Jude copied the blessing into a journal for his dad and his sister. The blessing begins, "Jude, I love you a lot and Jesus loves you even more than I do! I am very pleased with you and I am so glad you are my son. You are God's beloved child, and he is pleased with you . . ." Jude painstakingly copied this blessing twice, swapping out references to himself and inserting his dad and his sister: "I am so glad you are my dad" and "I am so glad you are my sister."

Out of an increased affection for Jesus, Jude's spiritual journey—Upward, Inward, Outward, and Withward—began to blossom. And, putting a perfect bow on our conversation about the Affiliative-aged child's increased identification with the faith community, several times that day he told his dad this: "I want to be just like you, dad. You have a strong relationship with God, and I want that."[10]

AFFILIATIVE STAGE PRACTICES

Note that because each stage transcends and includes the previous stages, many of the Experiential practices are still great options.

Up: Being with Jesus.

- Practice prayer journaling.

- Create a special God time nook.

- Draw, paint, dance, or play an instrument while listening to worship music.

- Read and sing along with worship lyrics at church.

- Read a daily devotional such as *Jesus Calling: 365 Devotions for Kids*.

- Experiment with Ignatian Bible study. Invite children to use their imaginations to put themselves in a Bible story. What do they see? What do they hear? What does it feel like?

- Purchase an "older kid" Bible at this stage if you haven't already. *The Action Bible* and *The NIV Action Study Bible* are wonderful. I am aware that they are marketed to boys, but please buy them for your girls as well.

- Try inductive Bible study. Study the passage like a detective.

In: Becoming like Jesus.

- Help the child confess their sin to God rather than to their parents. Modeled on the "apology liturgy" from the Experiential stage, this becomes, "I'm sorry God for X." *What do you think he says back to you?* "I love you and I forgive you."

- Help the child learn to identify thoughts that are from God versus thoughts from the enemy. Use Scripture memory to extinguish "fiery darts" (Ephesians 6:16 KJV). Send bad thoughts to jail (see 2 Corinthians 10:5).

- Help the child learn to identify temptation, manage anxiety, etc. through a growing self-awareness of their inner life and thoughts.

Out: Doing what Jesus did.

- Respond to and agree with compassionate and merciful instincts, even if it stretches us financially, makes us feel awkward, etc.
- Involve the child in giving decisions as appropriate.
- Pray for disasters, tragedies, and notable news events. Consider responding as a family.
- Invite friends from school who don't know Jesus to church. "How do you think your friends who don't know Jesus could hear about him? Any ideas?"
- Ask the child to think of someone to intercede for at bedtime—whoever comes to mind—and tell that person the next day.

With: Following Jesus together.

- Intentionally identify your child's "five"—five adults who know Jesus and are intentionally involved in your child's life.
- Pursue experiences like PreTeen Boy Squad, Papi Bible Study, or both.
- Involve kids in corporate worship roles at church (serving Communion, greeting, set up, etc.).
- Share daily prayer requests at breakfast with the family. "What do you need Jesus' help with today?" Everyone answers. Pray together. Then report at dinner time and give thanks.
- Share about your own relationship with Jesus, your personal growth and learning, even what *you* learned about in church today (instead of only asking about what they learned).
- Plan or participate in father/son or mother/daughter events.
- Initiate solo walk-and-talks.
- Practice a dinnertime devotional, God hunt, or examen.

- Attend family camp, send the child to a trusted Christian overnight summer camp, or both.
- Help the child participate in a church choir, dance team, or drama team.

QUESTIONS FOR REFLECTION

1. Spend a few minutes thinking about any of your children currently in this stage. Acknowledge and thank God for the faith you see growing and developing in them. What do you appreciate most about how they relate to God?

2. What are your favorite things about this stage? What do you enjoy the most about this stage as you parent? What things about this stage can make discipleship enjoyable or fun?

3. What are the challenges of this stage? What are your least favorite aspects of parenting through this stage? What about this stage can make discipleship challenging?

4. Each of Westerhoff's stages is present in adult, Owned faith. Take a moment to evaluate how Affiliative faith has shaped your own spiritual journey: How strong is your sense of belonging to a community of faith? Who are your closest spiritual friends? How has God spoken to you through his people?

5. What is one new practice you'd like to try with your Affiliative-aged child?

For pastors and church leaders

1. How would you describe your church's ministry to Affiliative-aged kids? How does your programming encourage the "believing by belonging" mindset?

2. How are you supporting parents of Affiliative-aged kids?

9

AGES TWELVE TO EIGHTEEN AND BEYOND

The Searching and Owned Stages (or Please Don't Freak Out)

> *Doubt isn't the opposite of faith; it is an element of faith.*
>
> **PAUL TILLICH, *DYNAMICS OF FAITH***

> *If you would be a real seeker after truth, it is necessary that at least once in your life you doubt, as far as possible, all things.*
>
> **RENÉ DESCARTES, *PRINCIPLES OF PHILOSOPHY***

> *You will seek me and find me when you seek me with all your heart.*
>
> **JEREMIAH 29:13**

N THIRTEEN YEARS OF CAMPUS MINISTRY, I can't tell you the number of times my heart was broken by an eager first-year student who signed up for InterVarsity at the club fair, told me all about their high school youth group, and promptly ghosted us two to three weeks later. This happened over and over. Sometimes I'd run into them on Thursday nights after fellowship gatherings, stumbling back to their dorm rooms, suddenly engrossed by something on their phone (thus leaving no chance for eye contact). These are the 50 percent, dedicated youth group kids who thrived in the Affiliative stage but are now struggling to follow Jesus as emerging adults. Why? Well, it's quite possible they skipped the Searching stage entirely. Westerhoff's stages help us identify another wrong turn in answer to the "How did we get here?" question from chapter one: how the church has often dealt with doubt and questioning. To unpack this, we'll look at the Searching and Owned stages side-by-side in this chapter.

SEARCHING: AGES TWELVE TO EIGHTEEN

When I was thirteen, in preparation for an epic two-month cross-country family road trip, my dad traded in his cute blue Hyundai with the sunroof for a giant, mustard yellow twelve-passenger van. It was ugly and embarrassing enough in all its yellow diesel glory. But then, that spring, Dad decided to turn it into a rolling billboard for Easter services at the church he was pastoring. He bought some glass markers and proceeded to cover the windows with the following:

Left: CHRIST HAS DIED *picture of three crosses*

Back: CHRIST HAS RISEN *picture of an empty tomb*

Right: CHRIST WILL COME AGAIN *picture of Jesus descending from the clouds*

As you may have guessed by now, I model a lot of my discipleship habits after my own parents. But if your goal is to build a sense of trust and safety with your Searching-aged children (especially if you are the one who drops them off at middle school every morning), this is not a strategy I will be recommending.

For middle and high school students, the primary mode of spiritual engagement is questioning. In this stage, the child moves from a communal understanding of faith to a personal understanding. And the process of questioning is an essential prerequisite for independent discovery, internalized belief, and mature decision-making.

My friends Julian and Sera describe how they have seen this searching play out differently in each of their daughters, based on their personalities:

> Our older daughter, who is eighteen, experiences questioning around relationships and connections: questions about sexuality, race, ethnicity, and what makes for good human connections. And these questions overlap with her faith because faith is harder to talk about in high school than sex. But our younger daughter, who is sixteen, is far more interested in reason and morals. She is legit interested in moral philosophy, biology, physics—why the world works the way it does. She asks questions like, Can we trust the Bible as a source document? What about other faith traditions? So she's experienced searching in a more classical-apologetics way because of her interests. But her older sister couldn't care less about that.[1]

If you're starting to sweat just reading these words, you are not alone. This is often a troubling stage for parents. It's important to remember that while questioning *can* result in a loss of faith, shutting down or skipping this questioning can also result in a loss of faith. Questioning is an essential step in the journey to a mature, adult, Owned faith. Our kids cannot follow Jesus as adults without making an informed, independent decision. So as difficult as it may be to watch our children question things they've accepted as a given before or ask questions we don't know how to answer, we will need to guard ourselves against fear during this stage.

Because my oldest child is only just peeking into the Searching stage this year, I asked friends with teenagers how they keep their own anxiety at bay during the Searching stage. Here is what a couple of them said:

> **Rick Jakubowski:** I grew up in a Christian culture with a strong instinct to "defend the faith"—but I've had those conversations my whole life and I know where they go. As I reflect on how my wife and I have discipled our daughters, I trust they know the Scriptures, they know the truth, they have the biblical narrative in their heart. And now in this stage they are watching and testing out how this faith is embodied and practiced; they want to see these truths backed up. So I do my best to let them process and fend off the defensiveness. I leave room for mystery and not having every answer at every moment. Honestly, as they prepare to leave our house and go off to college, I remind myself that they may have years where they are the prodigal son in the pig trough somewhere, but the Father is still there. We are trusting and holding onto Proverbs 22:6: "Train up a child in the way [she] should go, . . . and [she] will not depart from it" (ESV).[2]

> **Jason Gaboury:** You can't give away what you don't have. If you want your kids to have a life with God, you need to have a life with God. I know that sounds so simple, but I try to cultivate a life with God. And in that life with God, I have to name my fears and anxieties and bring them to the Lord.
>
> For me, these two spiritual disciplines are helpful in cultivating a lack of anxiety: The practice of gratitude, listing

out all the things for which I'm grateful. And combined with that, zooming out and getting perspective on the whole of my spiritual life and being able to look for the hand of God. Because if God's been faithful to me through all of that, God will be faithful to my kids.

Last, one fundamental belief I have is there are no guarantees in the Christian life. There's no guarantee that my kids are going to follow Jesus. I really want them to, but there's no guarantee that's going to happen. And that frees me from a sense of responsibility for their life—it's not all on me in that sense. But it also frees me to say, if I want this, then I want to pursue it with them. I want to pursue life with God with them.[3]

I encourage you to resist two specific things during this stage. First, shutting down questions ("Why would you even ask that?"), responding critically ("Who put that idea in your head?") or with contempt (eye rolls, heavy sighs, etc.). These responses can unhelpfully attach feelings of shame to the experience of wrestling with questions that could instead be the key to unlocking the child's independent, adult faith. When we respond this way, usually out of fear, the child begins to feel guilty or unfaithful for asking or even thinking such things. Often, they simply decide to take their questions somewhere else where the sages of the post-Christian milieu will be happy to provide them with lots of satisfying (but ultimately bankrupt) answers.

On the other hand, as Rick alluded to with his instinct to "defend the faith," I'd also encourage us to resist answering our teens' questions too quickly with all kinds of facts and information or things to read. This may be something that God uses in their process—and some kids may respond well to this strategy—but giving teens a little more space to wrestle, and to interact directly with God around their questions, will often yield better results.

Julian puts it this way:

Sera and I have just tried to be in the conversation with them. We want to cultivate their questions and their curiosity, which we began doing long before high school. We want to create a space where if they've got a question—maybe it's articulated differently than we would have said it, or maybe some presuppositions are different from ours—we are not going to be anxious about that. Instead, we want to create space where we say, "That's a totally fine question. Let's think about that together." And we did have to work through some trust-building around that, because when kids are moving into the Searching stage and you have a strong perspective on Christian faith as a parent and as an authority figure, they naturally see you as the keeper of that box. They assume that you aren't going to think their questions are okay. So sometimes there are things to work through, but the goal is making it safe for them to ask questions.[4]

Thinking back to the God-moment framework, a teenager asking a deep, searching question about their faith absolutely qualifies as a God moment.

Part of emerging from these questions will involve clarified Belief, for sure, but leaning on Encounter and Praxis all the more heavily in these moments is critical.

What our teenagers think about God is crucial. But so is how they feel about him. When we shove information at them, we miss an opportunity to facilitate a relational encounter. If your teen trusts you enough to share their questions and doubts with you, see if you can encourage them to voice these things directly to God. God is not afraid of their questions—or yours for that matter. Remember, the goal is to shift from the role of mediator to that of facilitator whenever possible. For example, you could pause the conversation to invite them to simply tell God they are

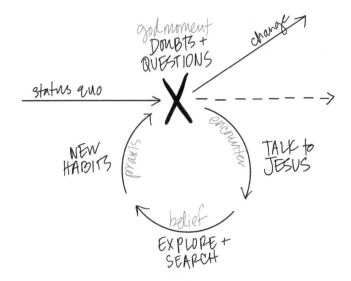

frustrated, confused, or angry with him. Even that simple act, and the permission to share negative feelings with God, may be helpful. You could also encourage them to write their doubts or grievances in the form of a letter written directly to God. Helping our questioning teens to engage their hearts through Encounter, in addition to their minds as they wrestle through what they believe, is essential as they transition to an independent relationship with Jesus.

In terms of encouraging Praxis amid questioning, consider what resides in your Circle of Influence during this stage. Though this circle is smaller now than it was when they were three, it has not disappeared entirely. During this stage, we empower and equip our children with the tools they need to evaluate—safely and confidently, without fear—inherited values and beliefs so they can make mature faith decisions. Your Circle of Influence includes leaning on the Withward direction through this stage, and even directly engaging your child's "five" for support and reinforcement. Encouraging your teen to bond and connect with other adult mentors and Christian role models is often beneficial during this phase, as is encouraging peer-based experiences like youth groups, retreats, and conferences.

When I was a high school freshman, I experienced a relatively short but intense season of questioning—not necessarily questioning my belief in God but questioning how serious I wanted to be about my faith. I was experimenting with newfound independence and self-expression (purple hair! ska! dELiA*s! new boyfriend! friends who could drive!) and my wide-eyed wonder about this whole new world opening up to me left me unsure about what it would look like to carry my faith into that world. To be honest, I felt it might hold me back from new experiences suddenly within my reach.

That's when Mary came into my life. Mary, a former Young Life staff member who had recently moved to the area, started attending our church. She was tall and blond with a contagious laugh and an up-for-anything adventurous spirit. Her daughter, who was my age, sported a buzzcut and was in a hardcore band, and her son was an artist with shaggy pink hair that he pulled into a mini ponytail on the very top of his head. I was instantly and magnetically drawn to them.

When Mary asked if I'd like to do a Bible study with her, I couldn't say no. She asked me to recruit some friends, and that was the beginning of our Girls' Bible Study. Over the next few years, we met every Friday at 6:00 a.m. for breakfast at a diner near our school. Mary listened to us, loved us, and took us through some classic devotional material. We could tell her anything. She wasn't intimidated by our questions or critical of our doubts. She simply listened and confidently pointed us back to Jesus. Mary and her kids also introduced us to Christian music and took us on road trips to music festivals where we bonded deeply as we camped and danced and stayed up late into the night talking. At one of these festivals, my best friend—from that world I wasn't sure could ever overlap with my faith—gave her life to Jesus. Mary was at the center of all of this. I trusted her, and probably even more significantly, I really *really* liked her. I have often said that Mary is one of the reasons I am following Jesus today.

My parents' role in this was allowing me to become close with Mary, someone they barely knew at first, and blessing me to explore and build an independent relationship with Jesus that they were not at the center of. I hope I'll have the wisdom and courage to do the same with my own kids.

LEADING THROUGH FAITH CRISES

So what do you do when your child is legitimately facing a crisis of faith or tells you they've made a conscious decision not to follow Jesus? I love these suggestions, written by my friend Jason Gaboury, so much that I'm going to let him take this section. Here are Jason's practical suggestions for what to do when someone you love has a crisis of faith:

1. Try an imaginative prayer exercise (on your own). Imagine sitting in a comfortable place in the presence of God. Now imagine someone placing different "weighted blankets" over you. Pay attention to how it feels to be covered with blankets of grief, suspicion, dissonance, etc. Imagine God lifting these blankets one by one. Now . . . ask God to fill you with empathy for your loved one. Pray for a healthy mix of empathy and perspective, compassion and conviction.

2. Listen to your loved one's questions deeply, thoughtfully, and without quick answers. Listen in such a way that your loved one feels seen, known, loved, and valued.

3. Affirm their questions. Mature faith is the product of doubt and disillusionment. I like to say something like, "I'm so glad you're asking these questions . . . it tells me that your

capacity to know (and love) yourself, the world, and even God is growing."

4. Commit to walking with them on their journey. Here's where a lot of us go wrong. We are tempted to try and "fix" their problems, "answer" their questions, and "resolve" their tensions. This fails to honor the loved one's boundaries. It's their journey, not ours.

5. Share how you've resolved the questions in your own life. The New Testament witness is confident, our witness can be confident too. (I've seen many friends absolutely nail empathy but then shy away from confident and honest sharing, afraid that doing so will be interpreted as "pressure.") If your loved one is sharing their crisis of faith with you, they want to know why you have confidence. Don't hold back from sharing. If you've not asked the same questions, or wrestled with the same doubts, find some people who have and learn from them what was helpful.

6. Pray with and for them as appropriate.

7. Practice patience. You can't rush physical maturity, emotional maturity, or spiritual maturity. You can pay attention to your loved one and actively engage them as they move through periods of growth.

8. Cultivate joy. Joy is indispensable as we walk alongside others who are seeking, searching, and doubting. We cannot manufacture joy, but we can ask for it and practice paying attention to it in our lives. (Joy here refers to the fruit of knowing and being known by God, not the presence of happiness nor the absence of sorrow, but a state of delight and gratitude in relationship with God.)[5]

Ideally, as the child moves through the Searching stage—and even potentially through legitimate crises of faith—our love, support, and leadership will set the stage for their ability to eventually experience an adult Owned faith. Let's look at the Owned stage next, with a particular emphasis on the transitions that are critical to reaching this stage.

OWNED: ADULT

This stage involves the development, either gradually or dramatically, of a mature, independent, adult expression of faith. During this stage, the child's faith has the opportunity to become central to their adult identity and all aspects of life. It is no longer merely faith inherited from childhood or the faith of the community, but faith that is personally owned and embraced independently.

All three previous types of faith are present in adult, Owned faith: Our experience of God and participation in embodied practices is still important to our understanding of God. Our affiliation and connection to the church and to other believers is still essential—the way of Jesus cannot be lived alone! And continuing to engage God with the new and increasingly complex questions that arise in adulthood is not only healthy but necessary for an honest, intimate relationship with God. In your own adult walk with Jesus, you may have experienced seasons where one or more of each faith type was activated in a new way. For example, I experienced a reemergence of Searching faith in my early thirties when I had a traumatic miscarriage. We lost baby Lily at twelve weeks when Noah was two-and-a-half, and I wrestled and wrestled with God to arrive at a better theology of suffering than I had prior to that experience.[6]

According to Westerhoff, most people never reach the Owned stage of faith development. In fact, he argues, the faith development of most children never progresses beyond the Affiliative stage. Some of the reasons for this are as follows. First, many mass-marketed Sunday school curricula emphasize Belief (right thinking about God) and a reductionist type of Praxis (good activity and behavior) at the expense of Encounter, direct interaction with God. From the time they enter Sunday school, kids learn to see "faith" as synonymous with going to or belonging to a church, and behaving in a certain "Christian" way, rather than belonging to Jesus through a trusting love relationship. The belonging-to-the-church concept is an important element of the Affiliative stage but is not adequate to sustain the transition in and through the Searching stage. Without a shift at some point to an individual ownership of the faith they've inherited, which is helped exponentially by interpersonal Encounter and heart-level interaction with Jesus, the child cannot progress beyond the Affiliative stage.

Second, the Searching stage often terrifies parents and churches because they are tempted to view questions and doubt as a *threat* to adult faith, rather than a prerequisite for it. There are few processes or support systems built into typical youth programming to encourage and facilitate Searching as a legitimate spiritual stage worthy of attention and even celebration. Most formal programming for teens continues to foster an Affiliative mindset.

This, in part, explains why 50 percent of high school students actively involved in their churches in high school walk away from their faith *after* graduation. High school graduation is the point at which many young adults leave the proverbial nest. As they do this, they are also by default moving away from their primary faith communities—the family and the local church. If the child's discipleship has been truncated at the Affiliative stage, their expression and experience of faith is still intimately tied to their faith community—"I believe because we believe." Faith that does not move from the Affiliative stage through the Searching and into the Owned stage literally cannot stand on its own apart from the primary community of faith.

This is why my InterVarsity experience of church kids eagerly signing up and then ghosting was so common. There was a time when we would joke that we were more likely to retain non-Christians in our campus fellowships than church kids. One missing piece seems to be helping kids make the transition from believing-by-belonging in their early teen years to an individually chosen and owned love relationship with Jesus by the end of their teen years.

Here are two other things to consider as we help our kids progress through the Searching stage into a fully Owned, adult faith.

INVITE DECISION-MAKING

When I was a young adult, I was often "jealous" of friends with dramatic conversion experiences. For example, Greg's experience of coming to faith was different, and much more interesting, than mine. He was raised in a nominally Lutheran home and attended church twice a year, on Christmas and Easter. Spirituality was not central to his family life, and he did not have a relationship with God in childhood. When he was in high school, however, two things happened: first, Greg tried to impress Dave, an older boy he admired, with stories of recent Halloween pranks he'd engaged in (involving eggs and toilet paper). Dave told Greg that he had become a Christian and didn't think egging houses was cool anymore. Second, shortly thereafter, on a band trip, Greg struck up a conversation with a cute tuba player named Danielle as they gazed at the stars. He asked her if she thought there was anything out there (meaning did aliens exist). She answered yes, told him about Jesus, and invited him to youth group. When Greg showed up, hoping to spend more time with Danielle, she promptly passed him off to Dave. The rest is history. By the end of that year, at age sixteen, Greg gave his life to Jesus and was baptized in a hot tub in a high school auditorium where his church met for worship.

My story was different. I was baptized as a baby. I can't remember a time I didn't know or love Jesus and can't remember a specific "decision moment" as a child. Like Westerhoff's model, I simply grew up into my faith, adding new rings of faith gradually as my relationship with Jesus matured. When I was sixteen, I participated in our church's Confirmation Class. For those of us baptized as babies, this was an optional experience designed to help us understand and own our baptism with a public declaration of faith in Jesus. I remember learning about the history of Christian denominations, about apostolic succession, and the significance of the bishop laying hands on us as part of this process. I remember learning some helpful theological concepts and writing out a personal statement of faith. I also remember the lavender skirt suit I wore for the service. I wasn't reluctant or resistant to this experience in any way—it all made sense and seemed like a good thing to do—but it didn't have much emotional or heart-level ownership for me and does not stand out significantly in my spiritual story.

What does stand out, however, was a Sunday morning worship service at our church with a guest preacher named Cal Fox. I was fourteen at the time. I had just met Mary and her family, and I was right in the middle of my angst about the new boyfriend and the new friends and whether I really wanted to continue following Jesus, who was likely to put a damper on all of that. Pastor Cal preached on John 4, the woman at the well. He talked about our deep spiritual thirsts, and all our attempts to satisfy them that leave us coming up empty. He talked about the deep satisfaction of the Living Water that Jesus offers. And he extended an invitation, specifically to young women in the room, to come up to the altar to say yes to Jesus' gift of satisfaction and thirst-quenching.

Before I knew it, my feet were walking me toward the altar rail where I knelt and received prayer. From that moment on, I was single-minded in my devotion to Jesus.

What is similar in Greg's story and mine is the element of volition—that is, a willful, independent decision to follow Jesus. For those like Greg who didn't grow up knowing Jesus, this milestone in the journey of faith is essential: Greg literally couldn't begin to follow Jesus without a choice to do something new. But decision-making is also essential in the journey of faith for kids like me who have known Jesus their whole lives.

In his book *Beginning Well*, Gordon T. Smith talks about "seven strands of conversion"—four internal and three external—that weave together as someone comes to faith. One of these strands is the strand of volition, or will. He says this:

> There is no true and lasting conversion that does not incorporate the will. An authentic encounter with Christ Jesus, whether it be a mystical vision or a sobering discovery of truth, will always lead one to action in the world, to a desire to live in truth and serve the truth.[7]

Providing opportunities for spiritual decision making throughout adolescence is critical. At church, public invitations to receive prayer, to say yes to Jesus for the first time or in new ways, to surrender new parts of their lives to his will, and truly opt-in experiences—like the invitation to be baptized if they haven't before—help to engage the will and propel the child into new depths of ownership and agency in their relationship with Jesus. In the home, you can be intentional about extending similar invitations in a truly openhanded way to help your child experience more of Jesus and his life.

Rites of passage, such as confirmation, are also helpful because they provide a neutral platform from which to initiate opportunities for decisions. In my case, confirmation was less spiritually significant in my personal journey than the spontaneous, willful, decision I made at age fourteen. But it's possible that, without that decision at age fourteen, this rite of passage could have been a space where a truly willful decision had occurred for me as I weighed whether I wanted to make a public declaration of faith.

For pastors, I would like to offer two quick side notes. First, I am well aware that many of us struggle with the idea of the "altar call." I used to struggle with it too (despite having made a profound commitment to Jesus because of one!) until I began making them myself. A couple years into my ministry with InterVarsity, we were confused and discouraged that we weren't seeing more students come to faith. We often blamed it on the "rocky New England soil," but at some point that year we began experimenting with inviting public faith decisions. We worried it would be awkward. We worried it would seem emotionally manipulative. We worried it would turn students off or turn them away. But what we found was that when we gently asked students who were ready to say yes to Jesus to raise their hands in their seats to receive prayer, they did. And those decisions "stuck." To help adolescents, college students, and adults in your church to embrace a fully Owned faith, these types of public decision-making moments can be incredibly helpful, and in my experience offer much more potential benefit than cost to your ministry as a whole.

Second, regarding confirmation-type experiences, the concept of confirmation may be unfamiliar if your church does not practice infant baptism. But designing some type of spiritual-coming-of-age or rite-of-passage experience for adolescents, whether connected to baptism or confirmation or not, is something to consider seriously. Many of these experiences major on Belief—on learning the theology and doctrine and history of the church and on owning a personal statement of faith. I am working with my church to help design a confirmation-type experience that also includes Encounter—helping our teens to experience the power of the Holy Spirit—and Praxis—sending them into the city to serve and participate in God's mission. Confirmation may be a giant "God moment" for these kids, so we would do well to make sure their exploration of this moment is complete.

INVITE THEM UPWARD AND INWARD

In the same way that Sunday school isn't enough to help the younger child learn to walk the way of Jesus, youth group isn't enough for the teenager. While Withward experiences are essential for the Searching stage, they aren't sufficient. As the child moves into adolescence, helping them to journey Upward and Inward on their own provides an essential foundation for that Owned, adult faith we want to see them embrace.

For teenagers who are following Jesus or are at least open to discussing their spiritual journey with you, one of the best things you can do with them is sit down and invite them to participate in their own proactive discipleship planning. Help them set their own goals for growth in each direction (Up, In, Out, With) and to choose spiritual practices to try on their own—perhaps one practice for each direction. This will ensure a balance between the communal experiences they likely enjoy and the individual experiences they truly need. For the resistant teen or child who is seriously struggling with wanting to follow Jesus, this may not be possible, and I'd direct you back to Jason Gaboury's tips earlier in this chapter.

In my own teenage years, practices like prayer journaling and the use of daily devotional guides were helpful and I enjoyed those, but my favorite solo spiritual practice was one of my own creation. I had a regular practice of reading through the Psalms and rewriting the ones that particularly resonated with me. I would write them out using large, bold letters, leaving space between each line. Once I had finished transcribing the text, I would go back and write my own version of the psalm in smaller, more delicate script in between each line, translating the writer's senti-ments into my own words. The end result was like a piece of art and I hung many of them on my walls over the years.

STEAL THIS IDEA: PSALM REWRITING

Ages: teens and preteens

Supplies:
- Journal and pen
- Bible

Instructions:
- Write out a psalm in your journal, leaving a wide space between each line. Some great psalms to consider if you don't know where to start are Psalms 1, 8, 23, 25, 27, 46, 48, 51, 91, 100, 131, 139.
- In between the lines of the psalm, rewrite the psalmist's prayer in your own words. Consider using a different color or style for your own voice.
- Read your psalm back to God as a prayer.

Even when we have reached the Owned stage of faith devel-opment, we never move beyond Experiential, Affiliative, and Searching faith. So it's critical for us as parents to continue tending to each of these faith types in our own lives. We need to continue pursuing experiences that help us to feel close and con-nected to God, using routines and rituals and habits to ground us in something larger than ourselves. We need to pursue spiritual community—spiritual friendships, regular worship, and genuine community that feels like family. And we need to continue to be honest with God and ourselves about our questions and our emo-tions and to commit to being life-long learners of God and his purposes. Leading our children through these stages reminds us that we are never done growing, and we will continue to expe-rience new facets and depths in our relationship with Jesus.

Let's return to the Grace/Challenge Matrix. Especially if you have teenagers, but even if you don't, take a moment to locate where your heart is right now. Which quadrant are you operating from as we talk about helping our teens move from the communal faith of their childhood, through the sometimes-rocky paths of searching and questioning, into a personally Owned, adult faith? How are you feeling about your role and God's role in this process? What do you need from God today? Take a moment and talk to him here before you move on.

SEARCHING STAGE PRACTICES

Note that because each stage transcends and includes the previous stages, some practices from the previous stages are still great options.

Up: Being with Jesus.

- Encourage Bible reading and devotional reading. Start aging up; take them to pick out a new Bible. (Their old children's Bible may seem "childish.")
- Practice inductive Bible study with a group of peers, adults, or both.
- Help them design their own Special God Time. What would it involve? Music? Art? Identify the child's devotional "style" and allow for variance with the parents' style.
- Listen to worship music and attend worship nights.
- Practice lectio divina or visio divina.

In: Becoming like Jesus.

- Read Christian books, including autobiographies and other stories.
- Experiment with rewriting a psalm.
- Practice prayer journaling.

- Practice a nightly examen before bed—shared with a parent or journaled.

Out: Doing what Jesus did.

- Attend mission trips and projects (with or without family).
- Tithe.
- Serve in the local community through regular volunteer work.
- Mentor younger kids.
- Invite friends to church.
- Initiate spiritual conversations with curious friends.

With: Following Jesus together.

- Identify significant mentor relationships with nonfamily adults—their "five."
- Seek out significant role models five to ten years older.
- Engage with youth group or find other safe places to ask questions.
- Serve at church—teach Sunday school, serve on worship team, volunteer teams, etc.
- Attend family camp, a Christian summer camp, or both.
- Attend weekend retreats.
- Practice rites of passage such as baptism, confirmation, or coming-of-age celebrations.

QUESTIONS FOR REFLECTION

1. Spend a few minutes thinking about any of your children currently in this stage. Acknowledge and thank God for the faith you see growing and developing in them. What do you appreciate most about how they relate to God?

2. What are your favorite things about this stage? What do you enjoy the most about this stage as you parent? What things about this stage can make discipleship enjoyable or fun?

3. What are the challenges of this stage? What are your least favorite aspects of parenting through this stage? What about this stage can make discipleship challenging?

4. Each of Westerhoff's stages is present in adult, Owned faith. Take a moment to evaluate how Searching faith has shaped your own spiritual journey: What spiritual questions have you been wrestling with in this stage of life? These days, what beliefs do you personally need clarity on?

5. What is one new practice you'd like to try with your Searching-aged child?

For pastors and church leaders

1. How would you describe your church's ministry to Searching-aged kids? Does your programming encourage the "believing by questioning" mindset?

2. How are you supporting parents of Searching-aged kids?

10

USING THE FIRST PATH GUIDE

(or More About My Love Affair with My GPS)

*Twenty years from now you will be more
disappointed by the things that you didn't do than
by the ones you did do. So throw off the bowlines.
Sail away from the safe harbor. Catch the trade
winds in your sails. Explore. Dream. Discover.*

**SARAH FRANCES BROWN IN
H. JACKSON BROWN JR.,** *P.S. I LOVE YOU*

*The first step towards getting
somewhere is to decide that you are
not going to stay where you are.*

CHAUNCEY DEPEW

I'M **NOT EXAGGERATING** when I say that the invention of the personal navigation system changed my life. I haven't met many people who have the same level of admiration and respect for their GPS device that I do. Just consider how this glorious gadget gets you from point A to B: (1) you tell it anywhere in the world you want to go; (2) it locates your starting point using satellites in outer

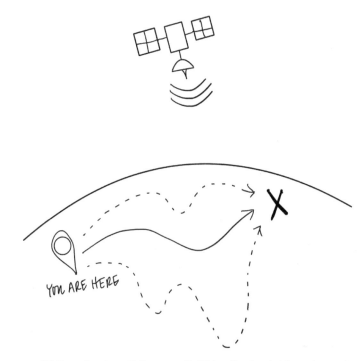

YOU ARE HERE

space; (3) it evaluates all the possibilities that exist to get you from here to there; and (4) it chooses the best route and walks you through it step by step.

Brilliant. Absolutely brilliant.

In the appendixes you will find two versions of the First Path Guide, my go-to tool for proactive discipleship planning. You can think of this tool like your discipleship GPS. The first version is designed for the individual child, and the other for the family as a whole. In this chapter I will walk you through the individual guide and how to get the most out of it. In the next chapter we'll discuss practices that can be done together as a whole family, regardless of age and stage, and you can use the Family Path Guide as a planning tool for those practices.

Each guide is divided into four sections, one for each of the discipleship directions—Up, In, Out, With. Each section is designed to lead you through a simple process to determine which practices might be helpful to introduce to your child's discipleship rhythms. I invite you to fill out one guide for each child so that you can tailor the practices to their specific needs, faith stage, personality, etc. (You can download additional guides at www.ivpress.com/teach-your-children-well.)

STEP ONE: DREAM

If you don't know where you are going,
you'll end up someplace else.

YOGI BERRA

The first step in this process, just like when you get in your car and plug an address into your GPS, is to choose a specific destination: Where do you want to go? Each section of the guide begins with dreaming, an invitation to access God's heart for your child through a series of questions related to each discipleship direction. For example,

Up:

- What is God saying to you about your child and his heart for them?

- How would you describe his dreams and desires for what their relationship could be like?

- What is the primary thing you want your child to learn or know about God this year?

This kind of spiritual dreaming exercise is different from how we often envision our children's future. How often do we ask our kids to tell us what they want to be when they grow up? Currently Silas wants to be a professional drummer, and Noah wants to be a writer or a filmmaker. When I was Noah's age, I wanted to be a park ranger.[1] But have you ever asked them *who* they want to be when they grow up? Or have you ever spent time praying and dreaming about this yourself? If you have girls, what kind of women do you hope they will be? If you have boys, what kind of men? What values do you hope they will live by? What kind of holy imagination has God given you for their lives?

If this exercise is difficult for you, I encourage you to practice the Ignatian prayer exercise I describe in chapter three. Find a quiet place, settle your heart and mind, and have a conversation with Jesus about your child. Ask him what he sees in your child, what his hopes and dreams are, what you should be paying attention to. Listen for his response.

STEP TWO: ASSESS REALITY

It does not do to leave a live dragon out of
your calculations, if you live near him.

GANDALF IN J. R. R. TOLKIEN, *THE HOBBIT*

We can't chart a course forward until we know where we're starting from. Just like the GPS satellites orbiting the globe work their magic of triangulation to pinpoint your exact location on a map, the questions in this section are designed to help you get a realistic sense of where, exactly, you're starting from. Factors like your child's age, spiritual stage, temperament, and personality as well as the reality of your family life will affect the eventual route you'll take to encourage your child toward the destination you dreamed about with God. For each direction, you will be prompted to reflect on the following questions:

- What is significant about your child's faith stage as you consider this direction?

- Considering your child's interests and personality; existing routines and rhythms; current circumstances and past experiences; outside constraints; and relationships with you and others,

- What things do you have going for you that might be relevant?

- What challenges are you facing that might be relevant?

Skipping this step can lead to attempting practices that, for a variety of reasons, won't work well for your child or family. I remember talking with the parents of a two-year-old about how they struggled to make it through their bedtime Bible reading routine. After probing a bit to find out more, they looked at each other and laughed as they explained, "Well, to be honest, Jesse rips all the Bibles." They had been using adult Bibles, with thin paper pages, to read to their kiddos. Out of a beautiful desire to disciple their kids, they had chosen a practice that didn't fully account for Jesse's reality. As we explored their specific reality a little more, they realized one thing they had in the "going for them" category was that both Jesse and his older sister loved music. So they began experimenting with some family worship time at bedtime instead, which was much more enjoyable for everyone. (I also suggested they invest in some Bible story board books!)

For older children, consider their spiritual temperament when assessing reality. Not every child will engage God in exactly the same way, just as they won't engage their peers or the world around them in exactly the same way. I've found the model below to be helpful as I have sought to better understand my own children.[2]

The Y-axis is a classic head/heart dualism and refers to how we approach God: Do we approach God primarily with our minds or with our hearts? Do we tend to think about God, or feel him?

To determine which approach best describes your child, ask yourself whether your child is more of a "thinker" or a "feeler" in general. We have one of each. Noah has always been a thinker. He's a prolific writer, reads almanacs and memorizes lists for fun, and tends to ask "facts" type questions about the world. This absolutely follows through to his spirituality. In the midst of a cover-to-cover

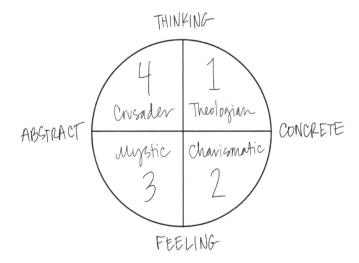

Bible reading challenge, he recently asked us to explain why the genealogies in Matthew and Luke are different. Silas, on the other hand, is what you would call "all heart." He is fascinated by people and relationships, doesn't enjoy reading for pleasure, and would rather tell you a story than write one. Again, this holds true for his spirituality: Silas experiences many more God moments stemming from strong emotions than from intellectual curiosity. He also once told me that of all the things he does well, the thing he is best at is loving God. (Who even says that?!)

The X-axis is designed to determine our experience of God: Do we tend to experience God as mystery (Spirit) or God as revealed (through Jesus, the Bible, etc.)?

This axis is trickier to determine for kiddos, especially for little ones who are more concrete than abstract by nature. But as they mature, they may begin to differentiate. Noah is clearly drawn to the concrete, to God revealed through Scripture. When he listens for God's voice, he tends to experience God's voice in words. And we think Silas may be drawn more to mystery, to God as Spirit.

Silas spends a lot of his prayer time thanking God for grand things like the gift of life or the gift of God's self. When he listens for God's voice, Silas almost always sees a picture.

If you are able to tentatively locate your own children within one of these types, knowing it may change and flux over the years, here are a few thoughts about each type that may be relevant as you assess your starting reality:

Type 1: Theologian

Head spirituality

Primary posture: "God is revealed, and I seek to understand him."

Favorite practices: Reading, Scripture study

Favorite direction: Up

These kids, like Noah, want to engage their minds in their walk with Jesus. Feed their hunger for understanding God with practices like Bible study, reading, and Scripture memory.

Type 2: Charismatic

Heart spirituality

Primary posture: "God is revealed, and I seek to emotionally feel him."

Favorite practices: Worship, small groups

Favorite direction: With

These kids want to engage their hearts in their walk with Jesus. Feed their desire for emotional connection with practices like musical worship, dance, and enjoying God in community.

Type 3: Mystic

Mystical spirituality[3]

Primary posture: "God is a mystery, and I seek to emotionally feel him."

Favorite practices: Silence, nature, imaginative prayer

Favorite direction: In

These kids, like Silas, may express a deep love for God or talk about him in ways that feel overly grand for such small people. Feed their desire for emotional connection to God through practices like imaginative prayer or contemplating a beautiful sunset.

Type 4: Crusader

Social justice/kingdom spirituality

Primary posture: "God is a mystery, and I seek to understand him."

Favorite practices: Witnessing, giving, serving the poor

Favorite direction: Out

These kids have a strong sense of right and wrong and a strong need to act. Feed their desire to be the hands and feet of Jesus by allowing them to serve, helping them tell their friends about Jesus, and giving them opportunities to be generous.

Part of maturity, eventually—and the usefulness of this model for adults—involves learning to stretch ourselves to engage God holistically, from each quadrant. My mom used to say that some spiritual practices will be like dessert (your favorites), and some will be like vegetables (harder for you to enjoy but important for your growth). As we're leading our kids, however, I suggest going with the path of least resistance: let them eat spiritual dessert for the time being.

STEP THREE: BRAINSTORM

Idea generation is about quantity, not quality.
Multiplication, not subtraction. Editing comes later.
The goal of brainstorming is to walk out with buckets
of ideas, not one precious idea perched on a pillow.

SAM HARRISON, *CREATIVE ZING!*

Once the GPS knows your desired destination and your starting point, it begins to map out route options. Should we take the highway? The scenic route? Are there any road closures to avoid?

What about tolls? The GPS does this in an instant, scanning the expanse between point A and point B for all the possible options.

In the same way, during step three of this planning process you are looking for habits and practices that will mitigate the challenges, maximize the bright spots, and produce the fruit you long to see in your child's life. Here are two tried and tested strategies.

First, don't reinvent the wheel! Borrow ideas from others who have tried them out before you. Consult your friends with older children about what worked well for them at various ages and stages, or brainstorm with a group of friends whose kids are similar ages to yours. If your child's personality is very similar to another child you know, buddy up with the parents to share ideas. Additionally, refer back to the lists of ideas in chapters seven through nine, which can also be found at https://sarahcowanjohnson.com/family-library.

Second, go ahead and reinvent that wheel already! Part of the joy and the fun of this process is creatively designing your own practices based on your specific goals and what you know about your kid. My friend Lisa literally dreams about new, creative ways to communicate the gospel to her kids. Recently she told me about some Holy Spirit object lessons involving balloons and dixie cups. There is no "set" list of practices and no "wrong" way to do this.

The goal is to come up with several ideas—"buckets" may be a bit of an overstatement in this case—before you decide which one to commit to. If you're the type of person who tends to go with the very first idea that comes into your mind, force yourself to slow down a bit and choose at least two or three practices to pick from.

STEP FOUR: COMMIT

Commitment is the glue that bonds you to your goals.

JILL KOENIG

The last step is to pick a practice and commit to it. Just like the GPS confidently lays forth a bright blue line amid the myriad possibilities, your role is to choose a single practice from among your many options and stick with it. Here are a few considerations.

First, check your influence. Refer back to your Circle of Influence to see whether the practice you've chosen fits neatly inside. For older children, be aware that some of this process falls outside your Circle of Influence and inside theirs. For example, "Have John join the worship team" might be an excellent Withward practice for your musical teen but is probably not something you can bring to bear without the teen's participation. Rather, "Invite John to consider joining the worship team" is probably the piece within your Circle of Influence. Again, for those who are not resistant to the exercise, I highly recommend including them in the planning process.

Second, when I say, "Stick with it," I don't mean forever. I mean long enough to give it a chance. If it truly isn't working well for you or your child after a good-faith effort, chuck it and move on to something else.

Third, consider introducing one new practice at a time. If you fill out the guide in its entirety, you'll be landing on four specific practices—one for each direction. Add new practices one by one, and only add more when both you and the child are ready. Learning four new practices all at once may be overwhelming and discouraging.

AN EXAMPLE

Here's an example of what this process looks like in real life, using the Upward direction and Silas, age seven.

Access God's heart and imagination for your child.

- What is God saying to you about your child and his heart for them?

I have the sense that God is utterly delighted by Silas—and even playfully amused by him at times.

- How would you describe his dreams and desires for what their relationship could be like?

I think God wants more of Si's heart—more of his attention, more of his love and wonder. His relationship with God is still mostly dependent on us—in this next season God will be inviting Silas to know him more deeply and personally. Also—Si's spirituality is not the same as Noah's. God wants Silas to interact with him as Silas.

- What is the primary thing you want your child to learn or know about God this year?

I want Silas to be utterly captivated by God this year—to know God deeply as a friend and to want to be in his presence.

Assess Reality

Consider your child's age, stage, and personality, as well as your family circumstances.

- What is significant about your child's faith stage as you consider the Upward direction?

Silas is just transitioning into the Affiliative stage. It will be important to foster relationships with other Jesus-followers aside from us. Papi Bible Study will be more significant than ever. Is there a way to help him bond spiritually with friends his age? (Richard, Juni, Harper?) We should reengage his godparents (Sarah + Shin) during this stage.

- Considering your child's interests and personality; existing routines and rhythms; current circumstances and past experiences; outside constraints; and relationships with you and others,

  - What things do you have going for you that might be relevant?

We have identified the 7:00 p.m. window as a time-frame we could maximize—everyone is home, no one is in bed, mostly we are just unsuccessfully trying to get everyone ready for bed. We could easily start "bedtime" at 7:30.

Specific to Si—he really <u>loves</u> God. His feelings about Jesus are positive. He has a vivid imagination and enjoys imaginative prayer. He loves being with us and doing spiritual practices together.

  - What challenges are you facing that might be relevant?

Si can struggle more with sitting still, being calm, etc. when Noah is around. It's much easier to encourage him + get his full attention when we are one-on-one with him. It's also too easy for us to shift the conversation "up" to Noah's level rather than tailor it to Silas when they are together. We don't want Si's needs, interests, etc. to be overlooked.

Brainstorm

Name some achievable practices, exercises, rhythms.

- What are some practices that could help cultivate the fruit you long to see this year?

- Independent Special God Time (creating a nook, etc.)

- Prayer journal or drawing

- Imaginative Prayer book by Jared Boyd - read this together.

- How could you maximize some of the things you already have going for you?

- 7:00 p.m. time - parallel special God time as a family. Maximizes that time, encourages all of us to connect with God independently.

- Imaginative prayer book would engage Si's heart and imagination and his interest in doing spiritual practice with us vs. alone.

- How could you minimize some of the challenges you are experiencing?

Doing the book w/ Silas alone will minimize the Noah factor. Engaging his heart + imagination will meet him in his particular preferences vs. assuming he will be just like Noah.

Commit

Only commit to things that are within your Circle of Influence and realistic for you to follow through on.

- What are you ready to commit to?

- Nightly 7:00 p.m. parallel Special God Time for the whole family Monday-Thursday, 15 minutes.

- Silas + I will read through the Imaginative Prayer book together, one-on-one.

SKIN IN THE GAME

Each section of the guide includes a segment called "My Prayer and Formation Goals." This is a space for you to reflect on what leading your child through your chosen practice will require of you. It's a space to commit to praying for your child and to reflect on ways that your own walk with Jesus will need to grow so you can lead with integrity. If that presses an automatic shame button for you, remember the Freedom quadrant. We are aiming for Freedom, the land of high Grace and high Challenge—where you know it's not all on your shoulders, but you willingly throw your full weight into the work.

I encourage you to revisit this planning process at least annually for each child—they change so quickly! But a quarterly rhythm is ideal to keep it on the front burner and allow for more timely tweaks and adjustments. It's also a great time to check in on your own discipleship goals that leading this plan has highlighted for you.

Finally, keep in mind that these practices should feel life-giving rather than burdensome. The Northumbria Community, a monastic community based in Northumbria, England, has some helpful advice about adopting a rule of life. A rule of life (think *rule* like measure, not law) is a comprehensive discipleship plan which is very similar to the type of plans you are creating for your kids. Here's what they have to say:

A Rule works best when it challenges us. It can't be so easy that we are not stretched: but neither can it be so demanding that we have difficulty even meeting its minimum standards. Otherwise it is likely to discourage us, and therefore to defeat its own purpose. A Rule is not there to make us feel good or feel bad, but to help our individual growth in spiritual maturity. If it becomes hard to follow, becomes a burden or causes you feelings of guilt, then give it up—it is not for you.[4]

QUESTIONS FOR REFLECTION

1. What is your relationship with planning like? Do you love it, hate it, or fall somewhere in between?

2. What is it like to dream with God for and about your child?

3. Are you able to place yourself in one of the four spiritual temperament types? How does this make sense of practices you are drawn to and practices that are difficult for you? How could you stretch yourself to "eat more vegetables"?

4. How would you describe your child's personality and temperament?

5. Are there any personal formation goals already rising to the surface for you as you think about what leading your kids through this process will require of you?

For pastors and church leaders

1. How can you support and equip parents to think and plan proactively for their children's discipleship?

2. What is your spiritual temperament, and what is the temperament of your church? What are the implications of these preferences for your leadership?

11

STEAL THESE IDEAS

Shared Family Practices

*You are a product of your environment.
So choose the environment that will best
develop you toward your objective. Analyze
your life in terms of its environment. Are
the things around you helping you toward
success—or are they holding you back?*

W. CLEMENT STONE

*If the family were a boat,
it would be a canoe that makes
no progress unless everyone paddles.*

LETTY COTTIN

ULTURE EATS STRATEGY FOR BREAKFAST." I distinctly
remember where I was the first time I heard this famous line.
I was attending a church planter training course, preparing to join
the pastoral staff of our church, and my friend Shaun Marshall
was delivering a powerful word about the importance of creating
healthy culture. Since then, I have often reflected on the ways that

the culture of an organization, for good or for ill, can shape the values, activities, and even outcomes of organizational life, often without the leaders' conscious awareness or effort.

The same is true for family life. When it comes to the discipleship strategies and plans you are beginning to formulate, it's important to pause for a moment and reflect on the spiritual culture of your family—and whether it's going to munch up your best laid plans before 9:00 a.m. Is the spiritual environment of your home conducive to helping your kids walk the way of Jesus? Here's a silly test: If an alien were to visit your home today, would they observe, for example, that the fabric of your family life is woven through-and-through with your shared commitment to Jesus? Or would they simply note that you have a habit of gathering in a church building with friends most Sundays?

Changing the culture of your family life might seem like an overwhelming task, and you might be ready to throw this book across the room and give up. If so, please take a deep breath and consider this: changing culture is often as simple as making one or two very small but intentional changes. In *Influencer: The Power to Change Anything*, Joseph Grenny says that "Master influencers know that it takes only a few behaviors to create big changes in the results they care about. To do so, they look vigilantly for one or two actions that create a cascade of change."[1] Hear me, friends: we are looking for one or two actions that will create a cascade of change. This is totally doable.

If increasing the spirituality of your family culture is something you want to work on, one of the best "cascade-creating" changes you can make is introducing a shared spiritual practice into your daily or weekly routine that everyone in the family can participate in together. Shared practices and routines, whether we're talking about family discipleship or job satisfaction in the workplace, can have an enormous impact on that powerful but often unseen force called culture. After making one small change to introduce a shared spiritual practice at dinnertime, my friend Deb told me, "It has changed our family to be much more God-focused all week long."[2]

In addition to designing practices for each child based on their age, stage, and personality, layering in shared practices is an important element of proactive discipleship—one that can quickly create this "cascade of change" we're looking for. In this chapter I am simply going to describe some favorite shared practices I've collected or observed over the years—so you can think of this entire chapter as a giant "Steal this Idea" section.

FAMILY SABBATH

This practice comes from the Mook family of Providence, Rhode Island—Andrew, Corrie, and their three girls: Harper (7), Rowan (4), and Keller (2).

A few Saturdays ago, I knocked on their door around 10:00 a.m. and was welcomed inside by the older girls. As I settled down at their kitchen table, Harper excitedly asked if I wanted a glass of chocolate almond milk. I declined, not realizing exactly what was being offered. She soon explained the significance: "Miss Sarah, we only have chocolate milk on Saturdays because we do quiet time on Saturdays." I asked her to explain the connection and she replied, "Because Jesus' words are as sweet as honey. But I don't want to have honey milk, so we do chocolate milk instead."

Chocolate milk on Saturday mornings is a pillar of the Mook family sabbath, which they observe every week from Friday evening through Saturday evening—a twenty-four-hour practice that has become an essential rhythm in their family life.

Sabbath for the Mooks begins on Friday evening. To ensure that both adults enjoy a full day of rest, they have become "legalistic" (their word, not mine) about not doing chores or housework on Saturdays. They do a "blast clean" on Friday afternoons to address any immediate clutter, and then all additional weekend chores are added to the calendar for Sunday afternoon. Corrie pointed out that there is almost nothing natural about keeping a twenty-four-hour sabbath as a young family, so this militant prep work is their way of "fighting for it." (The Mooks have chosen Friday to Saturday partly because Andrew is a pastor and has church-related commitments on Sundays. If you want to steal this practice and can keep a sabbath from Saturday to Sunday, you could attempt to finish all weekend chores ahead of time.)

The Friday night meal kicks off sabbath in earnest, with homemade pizza and all phones and devices stashed away. At the beginning of the meal, the girls help light four candles. Each candle represents a sabbath value: rest, reset, rejoice, and worship. As they light the candles, each family member shares how they would like to embody that value during the next twenty-four hours. For example, on that particular Saturday, Rowan was planning to rest by "lying down and watching a little show" in her jammies, and Harper was planning to rejoice by playing Candy Land. Andrew explained that the "reset" value is mostly for Mom and Dad and often involves a creative outlet, or even gardening if it passes the "not-a-chore" test. The worship value almost always involves listening to worship music throughout the day on Saturday and sealing sabbath by attending worship together on Sunday.

After the Friday night meal winds down and the girls head to bed, Friday night is typically a home night for Andrew and Corrie—with the occasional exception of a night with close friends. Saturday morning begins with shows in jammies while Mom and Dad try to sleep in, followed by pancakes. After breakfast it's time for quiet time, the sacred tradition I stumbled upon as I arrived that morning. Harper breaks out the chocolate almond milk and she and Andrew sit at the table reading their Bibles and talking about what they are learning. Harper told me this is the time in her week when she feels the closest to Jesus.

While this is happening, Corrie and Rowan might read a Bible story on the couch, and Keller is probably toddling around with a teacup somewhere. (Lest you think these are mythical unicorn children who always behave and this scene looks like something from a Precious Moments figurine, I can attest that my voice memo of our conversation contains plenty of fussing and whining and normal-kid stuff as well. These are absolutely normal, human children.) After quiet time, the rest of the day is spent resting, rejoicing (playing), resetting, and worshiping. Phones remain off (Harper, age seven, has permission to police this), and social engagements are limited.

Reflecting on how this practice has shaped them and produced fruit in the life of their family, Andrew and Corrie talked about how much the kids look forward to sabbath as their favorite day of the week. Yes, they love pizza and pancakes, and yes, they relish having the full, undivided attention and presence of their parents—but more than that, Andrew senses that sabbath is forming their family in significant ways:

> We are creating culture. We want to follow Jesus into a day that is restful and fun and full of rejoicing—a moment that helps us reset for the week ahead. We want our kids to look forward to sabbath as much as we do and to feel its inherent value. We are trying to model and remind each other in meaningful and purposeful ways that we did not make the world and that it will continue to move forward without our efforts. Our family simply believes that sabbath is critical to helping us match the pace and rhythm of Jesus.[3]

Adding in a weekly sabbath is a much more significant change than some of the practices in this chapter, but the payoff is similarly significant. For the Mooks, sabbath has become one of the most important, cherished, culture-defining rituals of their family life. It takes work—this is why Corrie describes "fighting for it"—but you only fight for what you love, and it's clear that this has become a beloved practice for all five Mooks.

DINNERTIME CONVERSATION STARTERS

Once you graduate from the years of highchairs and booster seats and dinnertime chaos with very young children, the dinner table can become one of the best discipleship labs of all time.

This has been true for the Ondrasik family of Providence, Rhode Island. For Lent one year, the forty-day season leading up to Easter, I created a resource for Sanctuary Church families to use around the dinner table. Similar to an Advent calendar, but for Lent, this "Lenten Calendar" contained forty envelopes, one for each day of Lent, plus seven special ones for Sundays.[4] Inside each envelope was a small sheet of paper with three things on it: a short Scripture, a simple practice, and a conversation starter. The practices were designed to help kids enter into the themes of Lent: keeping sixty seconds of silence, silently confessing sin, and "looking for manna"—a practice of identifying God's provision in our everyday lives and giving thanks. Conversation starters included questions like "How does it feel to know that God takes care of you?" and "Why is it hard to be quiet?" and "What kinds of things do you worry about?"

Deb and Nick began using the prompts right after dinner and loved it. (For an added incentive, Deb added a small candy to each envelope.) They have three kids, ages seven, five, and three. Their oldest has a rare genetic disorder that has significantly impacted her development, such that her developmental age is around age one. So in Deb's words, "I plan these times for a five- and three-year-old, with grace that we also have an 'infant' present who will likely be noisy or cause interruptions and delays." They found that the kids really took to this practice—they were ready and eager and looked forward to it each night. Deb and Nick watched their youngest, who was two when they started, move from being "super disruptive during prayer time" to "always asking to have his individual time to pray, listing his family members and thanking God for them."[5]

So when Lent was over, Deb went ahead and made her own set of dinnertime prompts. Using colorful index cards, she chose a Scripture for each day, continued with the same practices that had been working well through Lent, and added her own conversation starters. For example, one of her first cards looked like this:

> Scripture: Philippians 4:4
> Rejoice in the Lord always; again I will say rejoice!
>
> Q: What are you happy about? What can you thank God for?
>
> Practice: Silent prayer to God.

The fruit they've seen from this one simple change has been significant—truly a "cascade of change" in terms of the spiritual culture of their family. Deb says this:

> Since starting this practice, we are all praying more: parents individually and together, with kids at bedtime, on the car ride to school, and throughout the day when things pop up. We have also noticed our kids talking about "God things" a lot more. It has changed our family to be much more God-focused all week long. And this was with very little effort. Because it was built into a routine we already had in our family, it has been easy to stick to.[6]

Two things made this small change work for the Ondrasiks. First, they attached it to a routine that was already working well for their family. This practice, called "habit-stacking," is a proven way to increase the likelihood of sticking with a new habit: you simply attach the new habit to another habit that you've already mastered. Second, the Ondrasiks committed to this new practice for the entire forty days of Lent, which was long enough for it to become a new normal for their family.

SIDE-BY-SIDE PRAYER JOURNALING

This practice comes from the Atwood family of Warren, Rhode Island. When Lauren married Matt earlier this year, she became a "bonus mom" to Matt's two kids, Jude and Cora, ages eleven and eight.

After attending an adult Rule of Life workshop, Matt asked Lauren for input in designing a rule of life for Jude and Cora. They had both found prayer journaling to be a helpful practice in their own walks with Jesus, and Jude was already familiar with the practice. As they began to establish new rhythms as a blended family, they decided to carve out a regular time for side-by-side prayer journaling. On the weekends the kids are with them, after a big Saturday morning breakfast, everyone retrieves their journals and meets up in the living room. Matt puts on some worship music, and Lauren sets a timer for ten minutes. Lauren says this about the practice:

> We hoped that this practice would help the kids learn how to hear God's voice by practicing times of quiet reflection. We also wanted to build in a practice to encourage the kids to share what was on their hearts honestly and directly with God, without us listening in or being the intermediary. Cora will often share, "Look at what I wrote!" but we never ask.

look at that facilitation

> Sometimes the eight-year-old says, "I don't know what else to write," so I suggest, "Ask God what he wants to say to you. And then listen." Sometimes the eleven-year-old

looks out the window for the last three to five minutes, but Matt and I insist they hold that quiet space even if they're "done."

The kids each have different approaches to journaling. Cora says the purpose of the time is "to pray" and often makes lists of people in her life she wants to pray for—everyone from Mom, to Grandma and Grandpa, to their dog Rhody, and even the trees. Jude, on the other hand, uses the time to "talk to God about my feelings," which strikes me as one of the most healthy and mature things an eleven-year-old boy could do.[7]

Lauren is up front about the fact that sometimes the kids' initial response to journal time is, "Do we *have* to?"

We respond, "There are some things we do together as a family because they're important to us. We eat meals together as a family. And we journal together as a family. I also love playing outside, and we'll do that after. Now go get your journal, please."

For us, it has simply become "what we do" on the Saturdays that we are home. The kids can journal and write or listen any way they like, but they need to sit in the living room with us until the timer goes off. I think it helps that Matt and I are with them in it. We journal at the same time, together.[8]

This is a beautiful example of creating family culture, especially as a brand-new blended family. There are so many other ways Matt and Lauren could choose to spend their precious every-other Saturday mornings with the kids. Spending time listening to God together is one intentional way that they are creating a healthy spiritual culture in their home.

To steal this practice, you can use the instructions in chapter five and simply choose a time where everyone, including adults, can do the practice side-by-side.

FAMILY BLESSING

When I was a child, Saturday night supper was different from every other meal during the week.[9] We set the table with the fancy dishes and linens, lit candles and dimmed the lights, and had a nicer meal than the standard weekday fare. But what happened after dinner is what made the experience stand out. When everyone was finished, Mom and Dad would push their chairs back from the table and invite us to come sit in their laps, one girl with Mom and one with Dad, for a Saturday night blessing. Even when we were "too big" to comfortably fit in laps, we never gave that part up—to Betsy and me, it felt essential to the practice somehow. Once we were settled in our respective laps, each family member would get a few minutes in the "hot seat" while the others took turns blessing them.

My parents began this practice out of a conviction that too many children—themselves included—grow up without hearing words of blessing spoken over them, particularly by their fathers. Blessing another human being is something of an art form and is often confused with praise. While praise is about doing, blessing is about being. Blessing is a way that humans image God. God is continually speaking words of blessing over humanity, most significantly when the Father blesses Jesus at his baptism: "You are my Son, whom I love; with you I am well pleased" (Mark 1:11). Sometimes a lack of blessing in childhood can look like rarely hearing kind words from a parent—or, in my father's case, never hearing the words "I love you"—but more often it shows up in a learned connection between achievement and affirmation. Parents often express pride and praise for the good or impressive things their children do—which is wonderful, and that kind of cheerleading is important—but when praise is not also accompanied by words of life about the child's *being*, who they are apart from anything they've done, the blessing deficit is similar.

Take a look at this chart below, which highlights the difference between praise and blessing. What all the blessing phrases have in common is that they begin with "You are..." Blessing speaks to who the child *is* and names something that is deeply true about the child themselves, not just their behavior. I'm not saying that it's wrong to use the phrases on the left and that you should eliminate them from your vocabulary as you interact with your kids. Not at all. I believe praise is important. What I am saying is to pay particular attention if you are completely missing the phrasing on the right, and work to add it in. In the margins, feel free to add in some praise phrases that you find yourself saying often, and think about how you could also incorporate blessing.

PRAISE	BLESSING
Good job on that art project!	You are so creative.
Thank you for offering to help me with the dishes.	You are so thoughtful.
Thank you for sharing with your brother without being asked.	You have such a generous heart.
I'm so proud of you for getting good grades.	I love the way that your mind works. You are so curious and that is an incredible quality.

Around our Saturday dinner table, my sister and I not only heard weekly words of blessing spoken over us, we also learned how to bless. It's not easy for kids to give compliments that are being-focused. Betsy and I often struggled with the exercise and, when we were adults, Mom and Dad laughed with us as they remembered our go-to blessing for each other when we weren't feeling particularly inspired: "Thank you God for Betsy because she's so nice" (sometimes accompanied by an ever-so-slight eye roll). You can help your younger kiddos learn to bless by asking, "What do you love most about your brother?" Over time, they will begin to understand the difference between blessing and praise.

Here are couple of steal-worthy modifications to this practice. The Marshall family notes that blessing makes an excellent birthday tradition in the form of toasting the birthday girl or birthday boy. (I'm imagining this could be done with fancy glasses full of sparkling cider and with lots of hearty "Cheers!" and glass-clinking at the end.) And my friend Matt gives each of his children a daily blessing. Matt has written Jude and Cora a specific blessing that he speaks over them during breakfast on the days when they are together, and he prays over them on the days they are at their mom's house. Jude says that what he likes most about this daily ritual is the way it reminds him that both God and his dad love him.[10]

The "cascade of change" here is one that Betsy and I continue to feel and benefit from as adults. This weekly practice profoundly shaped us. I believe that our deep sense of security and assurance before God—something we share that many of our friends struggle to "feel" even if they know it to be true—stems, in part, from hearing our parents' blessings week after week and, by extension, God's.

THE GORDON CHALLENGE

This practice comes from the Gordon family of Mystic, Connecticut. Val and Geoff have three teenagers: Sadie (17), Tate (15), and Kai (13).[11]

After a year of Zoom church during the pandemic, the Gordons realized their kids were struggling to engage—if we're honest, weren't we all?—so they decided to try some at-home practices to capture the kids' spiritual interest in a fresh way. They did inductive Bible study together for a season—which the kids liked but also said reminded them of their English lit classes. More recently they have landed on a practice that Val and Geoff designed for college students when they were on staff with InterVarsity in the 1990s. Called the "IV Challenge" back then, I've renamed it the Gordon Challenge.

The practice is relatively simple. They order takeout, and the whole family gathers in the living room with their Bibles. They read a passage of Scripture together and discuss. The goal isn't to do a "deep dive" into every nook and cranny of the passage like they would if they were doing inductive study, but to fairly quickly figure out how God might be inviting them to apply it to their lives. After the discussion, Val and Geoff issue the challenge: something simple, straightforward, and concrete related to the passage that they all commit to doing before the next week. When they meet next, the first portion of their time together is spent sharing about the previous week's challenge.

For example, the week I spoke with them they had studied Matthew 6:1-4, Jesus' instructions about not announcing your good deeds "with trumpets" but doing them in secret. They discussed why Jesus would have issued this warning and the freedom he offers from image-management and self-promotion. Part one of the challenge was to do something for someone in secret that the person may eventually notice, and then come back next week to talk about what the experience was like. Part two was to do something that probably no one would ever notice, including the recipient, and to keep this experience completely to themselves.

Thinking back to the "Encounter, Belief, Praxis" framework from chapter four, Val and Geoff are helping their kids lean into Praxis: to read the Bible not just to learn or to be encouraged but to put God's Word into practice. The Gordon Challenge is super easy to steal because Val and Geoff wrote their curriculum down. You can access it online in appendix E of the book Val coauthored with Don Everts and Doug Schaupp titled *Breaking the Huddle*.[12]

ALTAR BUILDING

This is a practice we have done with our boys at Thanksgiving, and I have often used it with adults as well. When Joshua led the Israelites out of the desert into the Promised Land, God stopped the flow of the Jordan River so they could cross on dry land. Once everyone was across, Joshua instructed twelve men to return to the middle of the Jordan to pick up twelve stones, one for each tribe. Then, "Joshua set up the twelve stones that had been in the middle of the Jordan at the spot where the priests who carried the ark of the covenant had stood. And they are there to this day" (Joshua 4:9).

Those stones were from the bottom of the Jordan River. Apart from God's power and intervention, they should have been underwater, completely inaccessible. Their very presence on the riverbank, piled up to form a monument, was a testimony to God's power and activity in the lives of the Israelites.

Altar building is a practice that essentially involves giving thanks to God, but the tactile nature of piling stones can be particularly helpful for kids. Additionally, the Joshua story helps us to give thanks not just for things we are happy about but for situations where God's intervention has made a significant difference in our lives. When we build an altar, we are giving credit to God for things only he could have done. This practice helps us to trust God for the future as we pile up a record of his faithfulness in the past. Watching that pile grow and grow can be a culture-shifting experience, especially if you or your kiddos struggle with anxiety like Noah and I do.

Ages: all

Supplies:

- Stones: river rocks are perfect for a one-time experience, while pebbles or small stones are best for a repeated practice

- Bible

- Permanent markers (optional)

Instructions:

- Read Joshua 3:14–4:9. Interpret the story briefly, translating it into language and ideas your kids can understand. For example: "The people built a big pile with stones carried from the middle of the Jordan River. Those stones should have been underwater, but God stopped the river so the Israelites could walk right over them. Every time the people saw that pile of stones—called an altar—they would remember how God stopped the river and give thanks."

For a one-time experience, such as on Thanksgiving Day

- Give each family member a few stones. For a dinnertime experience, you could consider setting the table with stones at each place.

- Go around in a circle and invite each family member to thank God for something specific. As they do, they can lay a stone in the middle of the table, making a pile (an altar).

- Use permanent markers to label the stones with thanksgivings (optional).

- Close in prayer. Thank God for his goodness, power, and provision.

For a repeated practice, such as the entire month of November

- Keep a small basket of pebbles or small stones on the table.

- Each night at dinner, give every family member one stone.

- As you pray for the meal, invite each family member to give thanks for one specific thing, laying their stone in the center of the table as they do.

- Use permanent markers to label the stones with these thanksgivings (optional).

- Allow the altar to grow throughout the month.

- On Thanksgiving, if you have written on the stones, read through the entire pile and give thanks together.

PRAYER WALK

Prayer walking—the practice of interceding while physically walking through a space such as a neighborhood—is a practice that can be helpful for adults like me, whose spirituality is more sensate and concrete than intuitive and abstract. Prayer walking relies on the senses to gather data for prayer: What do you see and hear, or perhaps even smell, and how does this help you to pray? For example, passing a school might prompt you to pray for children, or hearing a siren might prompt you to pray for those in trouble. For this reason, it can also be an effective practice for young children who are more sensate and concrete by nature. I often treat prayer walking with kids like a scavenger hunt:

- How many people can you count? Pray for each person you see.

- How many animals can you find? What kinds of plants and trees do you see? Thank God for all the beautiful things he has made.

- How many homes do you see? Pray for families and friendships.

- Do you see a park? Pray for joy.

The Marshall family of Natick, Massachusetts, found the experience of prayer walking to be a highly effective way to engage their three young children Lukas, Holly, and Benjamin—who were ages eight, six, and four at the time—in the practice of intercession.

Ryan and Andrea are part of a weekly discipleship group at their church. One week, as they were wrapping up, the group leaders said, "Same time next week, but meet us at Nordstrom." So, the following week, with kids in tow, Ryan and Andrea showed up at the mall to meet their group. After a brief reflection on John 5:19-20, and the idea that Jesus' mission was simply to do what he saw his Father doing, the group split up and headed out into the mall with these instructions: look to see what God is doing at the mall. Ryan explained, "Going for a prayer walk gives us the opportunity to ask God to show us what he is already doing in the places we already go."

So the Marshall family began to walk around the mall, letting their senses take in whatever they could and simply observing the people around them. Here's what Ryan says about the experience and the impact it had on their kids:

> We saw people having fun and laughing; having a terrible time and fighting; rolling their eyes at each other and at mall prices. We saw people eating, people meeting for the first time, people in arrangements that were hard to understand just by looking at them . . . are they siblings? Cousins? Lovers? Who *knows*?
>
> After about twenty minutes of walking and praying for those we observed, we regathered with the group and shared. It was an overwhelmingly positive experience and one that my kids recall and ask to do on occasion years later. It has also inspired them to pray for people in nontraditional settings like, "Dad, I saw someone crying as we were driving past. I want to pray for them." It's helped my kids react spiritually and with empathy.[13]

Ryan, who is a pastor, has noticed how few of the teenagers he works with are able to articulate the ways their families interact spiritually with one another. He noted that prayer walking from an early age could help normalize spiritual conversations within the family—in other words, this could be one of those culture-changing, cascade-creating actions we are looking for. Additionally, prayer walking is relatively easy to habit-stack: if you walk to school, to the bus stop, to the park, or simply around the block, consider adding in a prayer walk routine or prayer "scavenger hunt" as a way of normalizing intercession and spiritual conversations in everyday life.

I'm excited for you to steal any or all of these ideas because these are the kinds of small habits that quickly lead to a "cascade of change." With just a little bit of intentionality, we can begin to shift the spiritual culture of our family in such a way that the culture itself is working for us toward our discipleship goals.

Again, lest we think we can produce this fruit on our own, I'll remind you of Richard Foster's words: "We must always remember that the path does not produce the change; it only places us where the change can occur." But as we tread these well-worn pathways of habit and routine, we will begin to see Spirit-grown fruit in the lives of our kids. The stories in this chapter are full of such fruit: the seven-year-old who expresses a feeling of closeness to Jesus as she drinks her chocolate milk; the two-year-old who begins to pray; the eleven-year-old who heads off to school secure in God's love and his dad's; two adult sisters who share an unshakable assurance of God's love; the three teenagers who are putting God's Word into practice each week; an anxious mother/son pair who see a visual record of God's faithfulness; and an eight-year-old who demonstrates an automatic instinct to intercede for a crying child.

In appendix B, you will find a blank Family Path Guide to assist you in your planning process. What fruit could God grow in your children, and in you—what "cascade of change" could you experience—because of a simple choice to make shared spiritual practices a priority in your home?

QUESTIONS FOR REFLECTION

1. How would you describe the spiritual culture of your family? Would you say it's working for or against the discipleship goals and plans you've begun to identify for your kids?

2. In what ways would you like to see the culture of your family shift? On a scale from one to five, rate your level of hope that this change could actually happen, and talk to Jesus about the number you chose.

3. How does the idea of searching "vigilantly for one or two actions that create a cascade of change" sit with you? Do you have a sense of which one or two actions might be the most powerful for your family in this season?

4. Are there any ideas in this chapter that you want to steal? Or have these ideas sparked any ideas of your own? What's one next step you'd need to take to add a shared spiritual practice to your family rhythms?

For pastors and church leaders

1. How would you describe the culture of your church? How will that culture interact with the church's plans and strategies for equipping parents? In what ways will your church culture work for you, and in what ways will it work against you?

2. What are one or two actions that could create a "cascade of change" in your ministry to children and families?

12

FOLLOWING THROUGH

(or What Baby Squirrels Can Teach Us About Intentionality)

*The reason that everybody likes planning
is that nobody has to do anything.*

JERRY BROWN

WHEN I WAS TEN, I found a baby squirrel that had fallen out of a tree in our backyard. My parents called animal control to ensure there wasn't any rabies danger (there wasn't), and Mom took me to the library to read everything we could find on squirrel care (this was before Google). I built Timmy Tiptoes a little home in an old aquarium, nursed him back to health, and kept him as a pet for a short while before he eventually succumbed to his injuries (and my lack of squirrel milk—poor thing was not designed to eat cow's milk).

I have always had a deep love for wildlife and a special soft spot for wounded or helpless ones. Some animals I've rescued over the years include a bat that knocked itself out flying into the side of our house (yes to rabies danger—don't let your kids do that), a barred owl that somehow found its way into a college dorm room during spring break (the maintenance staff refused to help me), an injured snapping turtle stranded in the middle of the road (Greg helped and nearly lost a finger), a vole stuck in a window well, a baby mouse about to get run over by a car at Target, countless birds who have flown into our large picture window over the years, the occasional lost dog, and one very confused domesticated parrot who landed on our roof.

After years of being an amateur rescue ranger, I recently decided to become officially certified with the state of Rhode Island as a wildlife rehabilitator. I took a class, studied for a giant test, passed said giant test, received my certification to rehab baby mammals in my home . . . and then promptly failed to sign the paperwork to be matched with babies. There were some legitimate reasons—including the whole Covid-19 situation of 2020—but at the end of the day, I essentially failed to follow through on the realization of a thirty-year dream that was finally within my reach.

I imagine, in terms of discipling your kids, you have at least as much passion and good intentions as misty-eyed me watching a slideshow on proper feeding and handling techniques for baby possums. But even the most passionate among us may struggle to follow through on the best of intentions.

What makes the difference? What helps us move from intention to intentionality?

An intention can be defined as a combination of a belief and a desire. After receiving my certification, for example, I believed that wildlife rehabilitation was a noble, beautiful, even Christlike, pursuit—and I had a strong desire to participate. I had great intentions. Likewise, I hope that you *believe* (1) that you are the most significant influence in your child's spiritual life, (2) that you can absolutely lead your children and help them to follow Jesus, and (3) that talking about and practicing your faith at home is the single most significant thing you can do. And I also hope that you *desire* to see your children walking with Jesus for the rest of their lives. If these two things are true, you are walking away from this read with some good intentions.

Intentionality, however, is an intention combined with a few additional ingredients: self-awareness, action, and support.

INGREDIENT ONE: SELF-AWARENESS

There are three things extremely hard:
steel, a diamond, and to know one's self.

BENJAMIN FRANKLIN, *POOR RICHARD IMPROVED*

People travel to wonder at the height of mountains,
at the huge waves of the sea, at the long courses of rivers,
at the vast compass of the ocean, at the circular motion of
the stars; and they pass by themselves without wondering.

AUGUSTINE OF HIPPO, *CONFESSIONS*

Social scientists argue that a key piece of intentionality is the ability to be conscious of one's thoughts and actions; this is what produces the deliberateness inherent to intentionality. Put another way, self-awareness is a critical piece of intentionality.

Countless aspects of self-awareness will be helpful on the journey of discipling your kids. We've talked about several of them already: which quadrant in the Grace/Challenge Matrix you tend to operate from, your primary response to post-Christian culture, your posture toward spiritual practices, your own sense of intimacy with Jesus, and more. Just take a quick spin through the reflection questions at the end of each chapter again and you'll find several questions designed to raise your own self-awareness on this journey.

I want to introduce one final framework to increase your self-awareness: how your unique personality affects your motivation when it comes to creating new habits. In her book about making and breaking habits, *Better than Before*, Gretchen Rubin says "the same habit strategies don't work for everyone. If we know ourselves, we're able to manage ourselves better."[1]

Rubin goes on to identify what she calls the "Four Tendencies" as they relate to habit formation. These tendencies are based on whether we resist or respond to two types of expectations: inner expectations (from ourselves, such as keeping New Year's resolutions) and outer expectations (from others, such as meeting work deadlines). Using this chart, can you identify which Tendency you most identify with?

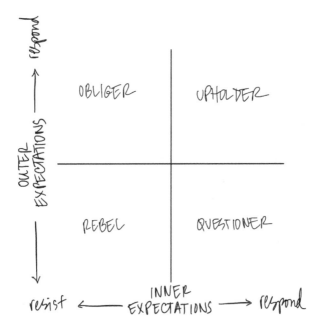

Rubin says this about the Four Tendencies:

Our Tendency colors the way we see the world and therefore has enormous consequences for our habits. Of course, these are tendencies, but I've found, to a degree that surprises me, that most people do fall squarely into one camp, and once I identified the Tendencies, I got a kick from hearing the people within a given Tendency make the same kinds of comments, over and over. Questioners, for example, often remark on how much they hate to wait in line.[2]

Based on your type, here are a few things to keep in mind as you seek to move beyond good intentions to intentionality in discipling your kids.

The Upholder.

- Meets both inner and outer expectations
- Key question: "What's on the schedule and the to-do list for today?"[3]
- Pay attention to: The Commit section of your plans. Don't overcommit!

Habit formation, while not "easy" for anyone, is easiest for upholders. But too many expectations, or unclear expectations, can overwhelm upholders because of their unwillingness to let any of their spinning plates drop. As you think through routines and habits you want to add to your family life, don't take on too much! Commit to one thing at a time and be ruthless in your simplicity and your clarity.

The Questioner.

- Meets inner expectations, resists outer expectations
- Key question: "What needs to get done today and why?"[4]
- Pay attention to: The Dream section of your plans. Nail the why.

Questioners are pragmatists at heart. Rubin says that questioners "respond to an expectation only if they conclude that it makes sense.... And they resist doing anything that seems to lack sound purpose."[5] If you are a questioner, understanding the why behind the practices you choose to add to your family life will be key. You'll want to pay particular attention to the Dreaming sections in the First Path Guides so that the rationale for each practice you choose is clear and compelling to you.

The Obliger.

- Resists inner expectations, meets outer expectations
- Key question: "What must I do today?"[6]
- Pay attention to: The support you'll need to see your plans through.

Obligers have trouble setting or meeting inner expectations but love to be externally motivated—especially by accountability. Obligers need a running buddy and thrive on deadlines. If you are an obliger, sharing your journey with others will be key. You could find one person to share regularly with or a group to process with.

The Rebel.

- Resists both inner and outer expectations
- Key question: "What do I want to do today?"[7]
- Pay attention to: Creating space for spontaneity and choice.

While habit formation is challenging for most people, it is the most challenging for rebels. Rebels are nonconformists who resist, or even resent, expectations, labels, and constraints—even those that are self-imposed. Rebels love freedom, so established routines and habits can feel limiting and suffocating. If you are a rebel, the key for you will be to give yourself the freedom to be creative and allow enough room for spontaneity in your discipleship rhythms. You may need to allow yourself to ask, "How do I *want* to disciple my child today?" You will need to be honest, however. If the answer to that question consistently becomes "I don't, actually," I encourage you to seek out support.

Understanding what motivates you is an essential element of self-awareness when you are trying to introduce new habits or routines. Without this self-awareness, you run the risk of creating plans that could absolutely work for someone else but won't help you specifically to follow through in a way that feels natural. Over time this incongruity will tax you to the point that the path of least resistance—dropping the habit altogether—becomes too powerful a force to resist.

INGREDIENT TWO: ACTION

Far better it is to dare mighty things, to win glorious triumphs,
even though checkered by failure, than to take rank with those
poor spirits who neither enjoy much nor suffer much, because they
live in the gray twilight that knows neither victory nor defeat.

THEODORE ROOSEVELT

The second ingredient that turns good intentions into intentionality seems a bit obvious. To move beyond mere good intentions, we need to *do* something. And yet, so often after an inspiring experience, we return home and, like me after receiving my certification, we fail to act. This is sometimes referred to as the value-action gap—the gap between what we say we want to do and what we actually do. Sociologists have identified this value-action gap everywhere from our exercise habits to our recycling habits. One scholarly article on the subject, by Dr. Mark D. Faries, is titled "Why We Don't 'Just Do It.'"[8]

So why don't we "just do it"? Let me suggest a few possible reasons.

Barrier One: We feel overwhelmed by the enormity of the task. Sometimes we fail to act because the task feels too daunting. Whenever I feel this way, my husband likes to remind me of that tired but somehow endearing old saying, "How do you eat an elephant? One bite at a time!" It's certain to produce an eye roll from me at first, but the wisdom of it can't be denied. Start small. Break the task down into manageable bite-sized chunks. Just start somewhere.

Consider using the questions in the First Path Guide as your starting point. It doesn't take much time to make progress. Andrew and Corrie talk about a time we were co-leading an event via video for parents at our church. I sent the group into ten minutes of reflection time, asking them to reflect on the "Dream" questions in the Upward section. It was almost 9:00 p.m. (late for Corrie), and Andrew had had a long day. They were tempted to enjoy ten minutes of silence on their couch. But, mostly out of a sense of obligation to the group, they pressed through their exhaustion to participate in the exercise. In those ten minutes, God spoke very clearly and profoundly to them about their middle daughter, Rowan. They rejoined the group, visibly moved, and shared how just ten minutes of intentionality had led to a significant breakthrough they would not have experienced otherwise.

This is how you eat an elephant.

Take out your calendar for a moment. Seriously, hold this page with your index finger and grab your phone with your other hand. I'm 90 percent sure it's right next to you anyway.

This week, can you find three ten-minute chunks of time to pull out the First Path Guides and walk through the questions step by step? Could you repeat that the following week?

If you repeated this pattern for a month, I'm confident you could identify a handful of doable practices that fit your kids and your life and don't feel overwhelming at all.

Barrier Two: We (still) feel inadequate. Another reason we hesitate to act is that we still feel like we're not up to the task. We look at other parents and have no trouble believing that they could do it, but not us. Our minds take the data we do have about them, whoever they are—that their kids are generally clean and well-behaved, that their Instagram photos are generally beautiful—and we fill in the blanks to create superhuman parents who have it all together and know exactly what to do at all times.

But friends, you need to know these people do not exist. We're all just doing our best. And when did you decide that your best wasn't good enough? Remember, you are yoked to Jesus. If one little boy submitted to Jesus could feed five thousand men (not counting women and children) with his lunch, shouldn't it follow that your best attempts at discipleship could absolutely change the course of your kids' lives?

If this is something you struggle with, I encourage you to spend some time talking to Jesus about why you feel this way and pay attention to anything he says back to you.

Barrier Three: It feels important but not urgent. Finally, discipleship sometimes falls in the important-but-not-urgent category of our lives. We value it, we see the importance, but the millions of other more "urgent" tasks of the day push it to the bottom of our list. Charles Hummel coined the phrase "the tyranny of the urgent" to describe this phenomenon. Too often we haven't allowed the discipleship of our children to move from the realm of ideas to the realm of our calendars or to-do lists. What could you do this week to make space for discipleship amid the many other "urgent" tasks of your day?

Pressing through these barriers to concrete Action—doing *something* proactive, no matter how small—is the essence of our second ingredient.

INGREDIENT THREE: SUPPORT

*There is no power for change greater than a
community discovering what it cares about.*

MARGARET J. WHEATLEY, *TURNING TO ONE ANOTHER*

The final ingredient that helps us turn good intentions into intentionality is support. If you can, I encourage you to find yourself a community of friends—perhaps at your church, perhaps a hand-picked group of friends on a text thread—who will walk with you on this journey, listen to you, challenge you, offer ideas, and pray for you. I cannot stress how powerful this type of support can be as you begin or continue this journey.

Here are some ideas to steal if you don't know where to start:

- If you are part of a church community that includes other parents with children at home, put some feelers out to see if there might be any interest in gathering for a one-time conversation about helping your kids walk the way of Jesus. Talk to your pastor and see if this is an event the church could help you promote.

- If a one-time conversation goes well, you could turn it into a short-term small group. And if that experience goes well, you might have found yourself a Parent Squad. Set up a group text or a messaging app channel or a Facebook group to continue the conversation in between gatherings.

- If you aren't connected to a church, or if there aren't many parents at your church, could you find just one friend who could become your parent buddy? While you are in the process of adding a few new habits to your life, you could consider introducing a weekly or monthly check-in with your parent buddy.

Finding your squad—whether a formal group or just one other friend in the trenches of parenting and as committed to discipleship as you—is one of the best things you can do to turn your good intentions into lasting intentionality.

CONTINUE AND CONTINUE AND CONTINUE TO TRUST JESUS

I first met Chuck and Debbie VanEtten when I was in middle school. I used to babysit their three biological kids, who are now adults. They also have two adopted children ages twelve and fourteen, have seven grandchildren, and have fostered numerous kiddos over the last decade including, currently, a four-year-old. All three of the adult VanEtten siblings are walking with Jesus today, so I figured Chuck and Debbie might have some thoughts about discipling kids. I was not wrong. Here are a few words of encouragement they wanted to share with the next generation of parents.

Debbie says, "Be intentional. Don't expect your church to provide the majority of introducing your kids to Christ. It starts in the home." Chuck and Debbie were proactive. They made a plan and they stuck to it. Debbie led the kids through daily devotions during breakfast, they prayed together over each child in their beds at night (out loud so the kids could hear), they protected a regular family dinnertime, and they prioritized monthly father/daughter and mother/son "dates." They also invited their kids into mission, participating in both local ministries to the homeless as well as overseas projects. The VanEttens made the spiritual development of their children the highest priority in their parenting.

Chuck says, "Create a strong family culture, but don't use that as an excuse to keep the world out." When Jackie was in junior high, Chuck and Debbie made an intentional choice to be "that house that all the kids want to come to." They kept the fridge stocked and made sure the kids' friends knew they were welcome anytime—and that the fridge was stocked *for* them. When the kids reached driving age, Chuck describes coming home from work and not being able to find a spot in his own driveway. But, he says, "I was good with that. I told their friends, look, if you have to get out, don't make everyone move their cars, just drive on the lawn. We're not raising grass, we're raising kids." The VanEtten family culture was strong—some might even say strict. The kids were not allowed to date until age sixteen, they had strong rules, and Chuck and Debbie "stuck to our guns." But they didn't allow this strong culture to become exclusive or to keep the world at bay. They invited the world right in, right to their kitchen table, practiced hospitality, and modeled mission alongside their kids.

Debbie says, "Lead by example. It's not just 'You need to do this, and you need to do that.' When we would do our own Bible studies, it would be at the kitchen table so our kids would see our own personal walks with God and see that it was important to us." They described explaining to the kids why they were not available right now: "Sorry, honey, I can't help you right now. This is my time with God." Chuck and Debbie prioritized their own intimacy with God, daily.

Finally, Chuck says,

Trust God. Pray, pray, pray! We've been incredibly blessed, and one could say "successful," but we don't attribute the success to us. Sure, we probably got a few things right, but we just keep thanking God. Because it's not always going to go that great—sometimes it's not going to go well at all!—but you just have to trust God with the outcome. Trust God with your kids' lives and do the best you can with what God's given you. Parents need to let their kids know that no matter what their kids do, right or wrong, that their parents are going to continue to trust Jesus. And no matter where their kids stray to—and a good number of them will—that their parents are going to continue and continue—and continue!— to trust Jesus.

Cheering our kids on as they raise our grandkids in the way of Jesus may seem like a distant dream to most of us, but that journey begins today. It begins with baby steps, theirs and ours. It begins with embracing our calling to spiritual leadership. It begins with recognizing God's activity in the lives of our children and with the intentionality to help our kids walk the way of Jesus in a world that doesn't. It begins with a decision to continue and continue— and continue!—to trust Jesus.

A prayer from the Book of Common Prayer:

> Almighty God, heavenly Father, you have blessed us with the joy and care of children: Give us calm strength and patient wisdom as we bring them up, that we may teach them to love whatever is just and true and good, following the example of our Savior Jesus Christ. Amen.

And now a benediction:

> May you teach your children well.

> May you embrace your holy calling to disciple the next generation.

> May you lead them by example, always growing in your own love for Jesus.

> May you catch the God moments that show up unexpectedly.

> May you lead your children with intentionality, creativity, and joy.

> May the culture of your family be fiercely loyal to God and open to the world he loves.

> May your children become resilient disciples of Jesus in an age that calls for such.

> May your prayers for your children shake the heavens.

> May you continue and continue—and continue—to trust Jesus.

> May you teach your children well.

> And may the blessing of God, the Father, Son, and Holy Spirit, rest upon you and your children and their children, now and forever.

> Amen.

QUESTIONS FOR REFLECTION

1. Which of the Four Tendencies did you resonate with? How will this self-awareness serve you as you begin to implement your plans?

2. Is there anything that holds you back from taking a first step toward following through on your ideas? Do you resonate with feeling overwhelmed by the enormity of the task? With feeling inadequate? Or with the tyranny of the urgent? What is one next step you could take to help yourself get unstuck?

3. Who is your squad? How can you engage and involve them in your journey of discipleship in an intentional way? If you don't have a squad right now, what is one next step you could take to begin connecting with others for support?

4. What have you learned about God as you've read and reflected on the ideas in this book? About yourself? About your kids? Take a moment to give thanks and to ask for God's help for your next steps from here.

For pastors and church leaders

1. How does your Tendency affect your leadership?

2. What support systems and structures exist for parents in your church? What needs to be created?

ACKNOWLEDGMENTS

To Mom, Dad, and Betsy, my OG family: Everything I know about this topic I learned in the discipleship lab of my childhood. What a gift to count you as family and as beloved friends. To Anthony, my new and only brother: So glad you have joined the ranks! Mom, we love you and miss you every single day. I wish you could have held this book in your hands but expect you are already enjoying it. In so many ways, this is your book.

To Greg, who has believed in me more than I've believed in myself: You are my hero. My encourager, my cheerer-upper, my writing Help Desk, the love of my life. I couldn't ask for a more thoughtful, encouraging, Christlike partner in life, in ministry, and in parenting. Thank you for midwifing this book into the world while I labored. I love you.

To Noah and Silas, my treasures: Gosh, I adore you two! You are truly exceptional human beings. Thank you for giving me permission to share these stories about our life together, for cheering me on throughout the writing process, and for sharing your faith journeys with me. You inspire and encourage me every day, and I am so proud to be your mom.

To Maureen Sharp and Shaun Marshall, who heard from the Lord about this book before I did and were bold enough to open their mouths: Thank you for your ministry of prophetic encouragement in my life and for the generosity you have demonstrated in sharing your gifts with me.

To Jenna and Michael Clouse and Andrew and Corrie Mook, who made this book better with your input and your suggestions: This book, and my life, would not be the same without you. With a shoutout to Adam Croft and the Applesauce Pigs, you all are the kind of friends people pray for—I know, because I did.

And finally, to Al Hsu and the entire team at InterVarsity Press: Thank you for believing in this project and for all your hard work to help me bring it into being.

All my love,
Sarah / Mom

Appendix A
FIRST PATH GUIDE

NAME OF CHILD: _____

AGE: _____

FAITH STAGE: _____

UP: BEING WITH JESUS

Dream
Access God's heart and imagination for your child.

- What is God saying to you about your child and his heart for them?

- How would you describe his dreams and desires for what their relationship could be like?

- What is the primary thing you want your child to learn or know about God this year?

Assess Reality

Consider your child's age, stage, and personality, as well as your family circumstances.

- What is significant about your child's faith stage as you consider the Upward direction?

- Considering your child's interests and personality; existing routines and rhythms; current circumstances and past experiences; outside constraints; and relationships with you and others,

  - What things do you have going for you that might be relevant?

  - What challenges are you facing that might be relevant?

Brainstorm

Name some achievable practices, exercises, and rhythms.

- What are some practices that could help cultivate the fruit you long to see this year?

- How could you maximize some of the things you already have going for you?

- How could you minimize some of the challenges you are experiencing?

Commit

Only commit to things that are within your Circle of Influence and realistic for you to follow through on.

- What are you ready to commit to?

My Prayer and Formation Goals

- How are you going to pray for the above? Be specific. How often, for how long, etc.

- Write your prayer goals here:

- What in your own life and walk with Jesus will need to change to lead your child through the above? Be specific. How will you tend to your own growth in this area? Write your formation goals here:

IN: BECOMING LIKE JESUS

Dream

Access God's heart and imagination for your child.

- How do you sense God inviting your child to grow this year?

- What fruit of the Spirit do you think God wants to develop in your child this year?

- (For older children) What patterns or habits is God inviting your child to turn from this year?

Assess Reality
Consider your child's age, stage, and personality, as well as your family circumstances.

- What is significant about your child's faith stage as you consider the Inward direction?

- Considering your child's interests and personality; existing routines and rhythms; current circumstances and past experiences; outside constraints; and relationships with you and others,

  - What things do you have going for you that might be relevant?

  - What challenges are you facing that might be relevant?

Brainstorm
Name some achievable practices, exercises, and rhythms.

- What are some practices that could help cultivate the fruit you long to see this year?

- How could you maximize some of the things you already have going for you?

- How could you minimize some of the challenges you are experiencing?

Commit

Only commit to things that are within your Circle of Influence and realistic for you to follow through on.

- What are you ready to commit to?

My Prayer and Formation Goals

- How are you going to pray for the above? Be specific. How often, for how long, etc.

- Write your prayer goals here:

- What in your own life and walk with Jesus will need to change to lead your child through the above? Be specific. How will you tend to your own growth in this area? Write your formation goals here:

OUT: DOING WHAT JESUS DID

Dream

Access God's heart and imagination for your child.

- What kind of posture is God inviting your child to develop toward the world around them?

- Are there any particular contexts (friendships, neighborhood, school, local, global, etc.) you sense God inviting your child to grow in their engagement with?

Assess Reality

Consider your child's age, stage, and personality, as well as your family circumstances.

- What is significant about your child's faith stage as you consider the Outward direction?

- Considering your child's interests and personality; existing routines and rhythms; current circumstances and past experiences; outside constraints; and relationships with you and others,

  - What things do you have going for you that might be relevant?

  - What challenges are you facing that might be relevant?

Brainstorm

Name some achievable practices, exercises, and rhythms.

- What are some practices that could help cultivate the fruit you long to see this year?

- How could you maximize some of the things you already have going for you?

- How could you minimize some of the challenges you are experiencing?

Commit

Only commit to things that are within your Circle of Influence and realistic for you to follow through on.

- What are you ready to commit to?

My Prayer and Formation Goals

- How are you going to pray for the above? Be specific. How often, for how long, etc.

- Write your prayer goals here:

- What in your own life and walk with Jesus will need to change to lead your child through the above? Be specific. How will you tend to your own growth in this area? Write your formation goals here:

WITH: FOLLOWING JESUS TOGETHER

Dream

Access God's heart and imagination for your child.

- In what ways do you sense God inviting your child into community and engagement with the larger church community?

- What kind of spiritual community do you long for your child to be part of?

- (For older children) What kind of friend is God inviting your child to become this year?

Assess Reality

Consider your child's age, stage, and personality, as well as your family circumstances.

- What is significant about your child's faith stage as you consider the Withward direction?

- Considering your child's interests and personality; existing routines and rhythms; current circumstances and past experiences; outside constraints; and relationships with you and others,

  - What things do you have going for you that might be relevant?

  - What challenges are you facing that might be relevant?

Brainstorm
Name some achievable practices, exercises, and rhythms.

- What are some practices that could help cultivate the fruit you long to see this year?

- How could you maximize some of the things you already have going for you?

- How could you minimize some of the challenges you are experiencing?

Commit

Only commit to things that are within your Circle of Influence and realistic for you to follow through on.

- What are you ready to commit to?

My Prayer and Formation Goals

- How are you going to pray for the above? Be specific. How often, for how long, etc. Write your prayer goals here:

- What in your own life and walk with Jesus will need to change to lead your child through the above? Be specific. How will you tend to your own growth in this area? Write your formation goals here:

Appendix B
FAMILY PATH GUIDE

Dream

Access God's heart and imagination for your family.

- What is God saying to you about your family and his heart for you?

- How would you describe God's dreams and desires for your family's walk with him this year?

- What are your primary goals for the spiritual life of your family this year?

Assess Reality

Consider your family circumstances.

- Considering your kids' ages, existing routines and rhythms, current circumstances, outside constraints, etc.,

  - What things do you have going for you that might be relevant?

  - What challenges are you facing that might be relevant?

Brainstorm

Name some achievable practices, exercises, and rhythms.

- What are some practices that could help cultivate the fruit you long to see this year?

- How could you maximize some of the things you already have going for you?

- How could you minimize some of the challenges you are experiencing?

Commit

Only commit to things that are within your Circle of Influence and realistic for you to follow through on.

- What are you ready to commit to?

My Prayer and Formation Goals

- How are you going to pray for the above? Be specific. How often, for how long, etc. Write your prayer goals here:

- What in your own life and walk with Jesus will need to change to lead your family through the above? Be specific. How will you tend to your own growth in this area? Write your formation goals here:

NOTES

INTRODUCTION

[1]See https://sarahcowanjohnson.com/parents-cohort.

1. THE BAD NEWS

[1]Kara E. Powell and Chap Clark, *Sticky Faith: Everyday Ideas to Build Lasting Faith in Your Kids* (Grand Rapids, MI: Zondervan, 2011), 15-16, 213-14.

[2]Mark Sayers, *Disappearing Church: From Cultural Relevance to Gospel Resilience* (Chicago: Moody, 2016).

[3]Barna Group, "The Most Post-Christian Cities in America 2019," June 5, 2019, www.barna.com/research/post-christian-cities-2019/.

[4]Aaron Niequist, *The Eternal Current: How a Practice-Based Faith Can Save Us from Drowning* (New York: Waterbrook, 2018), 94.

[5]Douglas F. Kelley and Philip Rollinson, *Westminster Shorter Catechism in Modern English* (Philipsburg, NJ: P&R, 1986), retrieved from https://learn scripture.net/catechisms/WSCME/.

[6]J. I. Packer and Gary Parrett, *Grounded in the Gospel: Building Believers the Old-Fashioned Way* (Grand Rapids, MI: Baker, 2010), 72.

[7]Powell and Clark, *Sticky Faith*, 32.

[8]Fuller Youth Institute, "What is Sticky Faith?" accessed December 17, 2021, https://fulleryouthinstitute.org/stickyfaith.

2. A LITTLE YEAST

[1]Jon Tyson and Heather Grizzle, *A Creative Minority: Influencing Culture through Redemptive Participation* (self-pub., 2016), 13.

[2]Jon Tyson, quoted by Open Door Ohio Church, "The Church as a Creative Minority," May 21, 2018, www.opendoorohio.com/open-door-blog/the -church-as-a-creative-minority.

[3]For more on this topic, I recommend James Choung and Ryan Pfeiffer, *Longing for Revival: From Holy Discontent to Breakthrough Faith* (Downers Grove, IL: InterVarsity Press, 2020).

[4]Stephen R. Covey, *The 7 Habits of Highly Effective People: Powerful Lessons in Personal Change* (New York: Free Press, 2004), 81-85.

[5]Michael Clouse, conversation with the author, May 24, 2021.

3. THE GOOD NEWS

[1] David Briggs, "Parents are Top Influence in Teens Remaining Active in Religion as Young Adults," *The Christian Century*, November 5, 2014, www.christiancentury.org/article/2014-11/parents-no-1-influence-teens-remaining-religiously-active-young-adults. See also Christian Smith, *Souls in Transition: The Religious and Spiritual Lives of Emerging Adults* (New York: Oxford University Press, 2009), 220-24.

[2] Please don't let my love of charts fool you: I have not meal-planned a day in my life, I detest the constraints of rigid schedules, and my work bag is a tangled mess of headphones and crumpled post-it notes. If knowing my Myers-Briggs type helps you to understand my point of view, I'm an ESFP. And for you Enneagram enthusiasts, I'm a 2w3. One of my favorite compilations of elegant, clarifying charts is Rich Wyld's *Theologygrams* (Downers Grove, IL: InterVarsity Press, 2017).

[3] Os Guinness, *The Call: Finding and Fulfilling the Central Purpose of Your Life* (Nashville: Thomas Nelson, 2003), 61.

4. RESPONSIVE DISCIPLESHIP

[1] In addition to being an agricultural term, the word *yoke* (ζυγός in the text) had come to be used in first-century Judaism as a metaphor for a rabbi's interpretation and application of Torah. That Jesus was likely aware of and alluding to this metaphor does not change the basic literal truth to which it refers.

[2] Adapted from Mike Breen and the 3DM Team, *Building a Discipleship Culture* (Greenville, SC: 3DM International, 2014), 51-66.

[3] Corrie Mook, interview with the author, November 5, 2021.

[4] *Evangelical* has become a loaded term these days. Here I am distinguishing between the original meaning of the word—pertaining to the gospel of Jesus—and the other associations it has come to acquire in our recent national political life (e.g., the "evangelical voting bloc"). From here on, when I use the term *evangelical*, I will be referring to the stream of the church that, flowing out of the Protestant Reformation, has historically had a high value for witness, personal salvation, and the authority of Scripture.

[5] A. W. Tozer, *The Knowledge of the Holy* (New York: HarperCollins, 1978), 1.

5. YUCKY HEARTS AND ASLAN ANXIETY

[1] Hallie Cowan, personal correspondence with the author, February 18, 2021.

[2] Lisa Olson, personal correspondence with the author, November 2, 2021.

[3] Hope Muller, personal correspondence with the author, November 6, 2021.

[4] Jared Patrick Boyd, *Imaginative Prayer: A Yearlong Guide for Your Child's Spiritual Formation* (Downers Grove, IL: InterVarsity Press, 2017).

[5]Corrie Mook, interview with the author, November 5, 2021.

[6]Corrie Mook, interview with the author, November 5, 2021.

6. PROACTIVE DISCIPLESHIP

[1]Hallie Cowan, personal correspondence with the author (postmortem), March 29, 2021.

[2]Jason Gaboury, interview with the author, October 26, 2021.

[3]"Christian" includes the categories Christian, evangelical protestant, mainline protestant, and Catholic.

[4]Pew Research Center, "U.S. Teens Take After Their Parents Religiously, Attend Services Together and Enjoy Family Rituals," September 10, 2020, www.pewforum.org/2020/09/10/u-s-teens-take-after-their-parents -religiously-attend-services-together-and-enjoy-family-rituals/ and www .pewforum.org/2020/09/10/what-do-parents-want-for-their-teens/.

[5]Richard Foster, *Celebration of Discipline: The Path to Spiritual Growth* (San Francisco: Harper Collins, 1978), 8.

[6]Aaron Niequist, *The Eternal Current: How a Practice-Based Faith Can Save Us from Drowning* (New York: Waterbrook, 2018), 4.

6 ¾. AN INTRODUCTION TO JOHN WESTERHOFF

[1]See www.instagram.com/stories/highlights/18045128116213768/ or www .instagram.com/sarahcowanjohnson/.

7. AGES ZERO TO SIX

[1]Cory Morgan, personal conversation and correspondence with the author, November 8–12, 2021.

[2]If you aren't familiar with Slugs and Bugs and have little ones at home, check them out at https://slugsandbugs.com/.

[3]John Westerhoff, *Will Our Children Have Faith?* (Harrisburg, PA: Morehouse, 2000), 91.

8. AGES SEVEN TO ELEVEN

[1]Based on what we are learning about the influence of parents, as well as the needs of the Affiliative-aged child, Sanctuary has begun shifting our programming for this age group from Sunday-centric volunteer-led structures only to offering additional mid-week spaces with high parent investment.

[2]Jenna Clouse, personal correspondence with the author, November 8, 2021.

[3]Laura DiPilato, personal correspondence with the author, November 8, 2021.

[4]Kevin and Corinne Fischer, personal correspondence with the author, November 8, 2021.

[5]John Westerhoff, *Will Our Children Have Faith?* (Harrisburg, PA: Morehouse, 2000), 91-92.

[6]Visit bibleproject.com to check out this resource.

[7]Kara E. Powell and Chap Clark, *Sticky Faith: Everyday Ideas to Build Lasting Faith in Your Kids* (Grand Rapids, MI: Zondervan, 2011), 101.

[8]Cheers to all you early-2000s nerds who understand this reference.

[9]Westerhoff, *Will Our Children Have Faith*, 92.

[10]Matt Atwood, journal entry, May 23, 2020.

9. AGES TWELVE TO EIGHTEEN AND BEYOND

[1]Julian, interview with the author, October 26, 2010.

[2]Rick Jakubowski, interview with the author, October 26, 2021.

[3]Jason Gaboury, interview with the author, October 26, 2021.

[4]Julian, interview with the author, October 26, 2021.

[5]Jason Gaboury, "What do you do when someone you love has a crisis of faith?" Facebook, June 4, 2021, www.facebook.com/505441676/posts/10158774306646677/?d=n.

[6]Lily has become a deeply important part of our family's story. In fact, one of the meanings of the name Silas is "the third." If you are one of the countless families who has experienced miscarriage or infant loss, know that you and your babies are seen and deeply loved by God.

[7]Gordon T. Smith, *Beginning Well: Christian Conversion and Authentic Transformation* (Downers Grove, IL: InterVarsity Press, 2001), 174.

10. USING THE FIRST PATH GUIDE

[1]Recently I've changed how I ask this question, to reinforce the idea that our jobs and careers do not define us. Instead of asking a child, "What do you want to *be* when you grow up?" try "What do you want to *do* when you grow up?"

[2]This is my summary of three adaptations: "A Circle of Sensibility" from Urban T. Holmes III, *A History of Christian Spirituality* (New York: Seabury, 1980); Corinne Ware, *Discover Your Spiritual Type: A Guide to Individual and Congregational Growth* (Lanham, MD: Rowman & Littlefield, 2014); and Martha Ainsworth, "Are You a Contemplative?" metanoia.org, 1999, https://metanoia.org/martha/writing/spiritualtype.htm.

[3]Traditionally, the word *mystical* describes a type of spirituality that seeks to attain union with God rather than, for example, greater knowledge of God.

[4]Northumbria Community, "Why Do We Need a Rule?" Accessed on June 17, 2021, www.northumbriacommunity.org/who-we-are/our-rule-of-life/why-do-we-need-a-rule/.

11. STEAL THESE IDEAS

[1]Joseph Grenny, *Influencer: The New Science of Leading Change* (New York: McGraw Hill, 2013), 62.

[2]Deborah Ondrasik, personal correspondence with the author, June 10, 2021.

[3]Andrew Mook, interview with the author, May 15, 2021.

[4]See sarahcowanjohnson.com/lent.

[5]Deborah Ondrasik, personal correspondence with the author, June 10, 2021.

[6]Deborah Ondrasik, personal correspondence with the author, June 10, 2021.

[7]Lauren Watka Atwood, personal correspondence with the author, May 18, 2021.

[8]Lauren Watka Atwood, personal correspondence with the author, May 18, 2021.

[9]My mom called the evening meal "supper," a linguistic distinctive that didn't transfer to the next generation. In New England, we call that meal "dinner."

[10]Matt Atwood, personal correspondence with the author, June 2021.

[11]Val and Geoff Gordon, interview with the author, November 5, 2021.

[12]Don Everts, Doug Schaupp, and Val Gordon, "Appendix E: Practical Challenges from the Putting-It-Into-Action Group," in *Breaking the Huddle: How Your Community Can Grow Its Witness* (Downers Grove, IL: InterVarsity Press, 2016), https://ivpress.com/Media/Default/Press-Kits/4491-supplement.pdf.

[13]Ryan Marshall, personal correspondence with the author, June 14, 2021.

12. FOLLOWING THROUGH

[1]Gretchen Rubin, *Better than Before: What I Learned About Making and Breaking Habits—to Sleep More, Quit Sugar, Procrastinate Less, and Generally Build a Happier Life* (New York: Crown, 2015), 15.

[2]Rubin, *Better Than Before*, 18.

[3]Rubin, *Better Than Before*, 18.

[4]Rubin, *Better Than Before*, 19.

[5]Rubin, *Better Than Before*, 19.

[6]Rubin, *Better Than Before*, 21.

[7]Rubin, *Better Than Before*, 23.

[8]Mark D. Faries, "Why We Don't 'Just Do It': Understanding the Intention-Behavior Gap in Lifestyle Medicine," *American Journal of Lifestyle Medicine* 10, no. 5 (September/October 2016): 322-29, https://doi.org/10.1177/1559827616638017.

BIBLIOGRAPHY

Ainsworth, Martha. "Are You a Contemplative?" metanoia.org, 1999. https://metanoia.org/martha/writing/spiritualtype.htm.

Barna Group. "The Most Post-Christian Cities in America 2019." June 5, 2019. www.barna.com/research/post-christian-cities-2019/.

Bayton, Mandy. "How to Live in the Tension and Grace of the Liminal Space." *Christian Today*, May 18, 2018. www.christiantoday.com/article/how-to-live-in-the-tension-and-grace-of-the-liminal-space/129256.htm.

Boyd, Jared Patrick. *Imaginative Prayer: A Yearlong Guide for Your Child's Spiritual Formation*. Downers Grove, IL: InterVarsity Press, 2017.

Breen, Mike, and the 3DM Team. *Building a Discipleship Culture*. Greenville, SC: 3DM International, 2014.

Briggs, David. "Parents are Top Influence in Teens Remaining Active in Religion as Young Adults." *The Christian Century*, November 5, 2014. www.christiancentury.org/article/2014-11/parents-no-1-influence-teens-remaining-religiously-active-young-adults.

Choung, James and Ryan Pfeiffer. *Longing for Revival: From Holy Discontent to Breakthrough Faith*. Downers Grove, IL: InterVarsity Press, 2020.

Covey, Stephen R. *The 7 Habits of Highly Effective People: Powerful Lessons in Personal Change*. New York, NY: Free Press, 2004.

Everts, Don, Doug Schaupp, and Val Gordon. *Breaking the Huddle: How Your Community Can Grow Its Witness*. Downers Grove, IL: InterVarsity Press, 2016.

Faries, Mark D. "Why We Don't 'Just Do It': Understanding the Intention-Behavior Gap in Lifestyle Medicine." *American Journal of Lifestyle Medicine* 10, no. 5 (September/October 2016): 322-29. https://doi.org/10.1177/1559827616638017.

Foster, Richard. *Celebration of Discipline: The Path to Spiritual Growth*. San Francisco, CA: Harper Collins, 1978.

Fuller Youth Institute. "What is Sticky Faith?" Accessed December 17, 2021. https://fulleryouthinstitute.org/stickyfaith.

Grenny, Joseph, and Kerry Patterson, David Maxfield, Ron McMillan, Al Switzler. *Influencer: The New Science of Leading Change*. New York, NY: McGraw Hill, 2013.

Guinness, Os. *The Call: Finding and Fulfilling the Central Purpose of Your Life.* Nashville, TN: Thomas Nelson, 2003.

Kelley, Douglas F., and Philip Rollinson. *Westminster Shorter Catechism in Modern English.* Philipsburg, NJ: P&R, 1986. https://learnscripture.net /catechisms/WSCME/.

Niequist, Aaron. *The Eternal Current: How a Practice-Based Faith Can Save Us from Drowning.* New York, NY: Waterbrook, 2018.

Open Door Ohio Church. "The Church as a Creative Minority." May 21, 2018. www.opendoorohio.com/open-door-blog/the-church-as-a-creative -minority.

Packer, J.I., and Gary Parrett. *Grounded in the Gospel: Building Believers the Old-Fashioned Way.* Grand Rapids, MI: Baker, 2010.

Pew Research Center. "U.S. Teens Take After Their Parents Religiously, Attend Services Together and Enjoy Family Rituals." September 10, 2020. /www .pewforum.org/2020/09/10/u-s-teens-take-after-their-parents-religiously -attend-services-together-and-enjoy-family-rituals/ and www.pewforum .org/2020/09/10/what-do-parents-want-for-their-teens/.

Powell, Kara E., and Chap Clark. *Sticky Faith: Everyday Ideas to Build Lasting Faith in Your Kids.* Grand Rapids, MI: Zondervan, 2011.

Rubin, Gretchen. *Better than Before: What I Learned About Making and Breaking Habits—to Sleep More, Quit Sugar, Procrastinate Less, and Generally Build a Happier Life.* New York, NY: Crown, 2015.

Sayers, Mark. *Disappearing Church: From Cultural Relevance to Gospel Resilience.* Chicago, IL: Moody, 2016.

Smith, Christian. *Souls in Transition: The Religious and Spiritual Lives of Emerging Adults.* New York, NY: Oxford University Press, 2009.

Sager, Alan. *Gospel-Centered Spirituality: An Introduction to Our Spiritual Journey.* Minneapolis, MN: Augsburg Fortress, 1990.

Smith, Gordon T. *Beginning Well: Christian Conversion and Authentic Transformation.* Downers Grove, IL: InterVarsity Press, 2001.

Tozer, A. W. *The Knowledge of the Holy.* New York, NY: HarperCollins, 1978.

Tyson, Jon, and Heather Grizzle. *A Creative Minority: Influencing Culture through Redemptive Participation.* Self-published, 2016.

Ware, Corinne. *Discover Your Spiritual Type: A Guide to Individual and Congregational Growth.* Lanham, MD: Rowman & Littlefield, 2014.

Westerhoff, John. *Bringing Up Children in the Christian Faith.* Minneapolis, MN: Winston, 1980.

Westerhoff, John. *Will Our Children Have Faith?* Harrisburg, PA: Morehouse, 2000.